MW00901584

MUSHROOM CULTIVATION FOR BEGINNERS

The Complete Guide to Growing Your Own Gourmet and Medicinal Mushrooms at Home, Indoors and Outdoors. | + BONUS: 10 Beginner-Friendly Low Investment DIY Projects

MICHAEL YORK

© **Copyright 2023 - All rights reserved.**

The content contained within this book may not be reproduced, duplicated or transmitted without direct written permission from the author or the publisher.

Under no circumstances will any blame or legal responsibility be held against the publisher, or author, for any damages, reparation, or monetary loss due to the information contained within this book, either directly or indirectly.

Legal Notice:

This book is copyright protected. It is only for personal use. You cannot amend, distribute, sell, use, quote or paraphrase any part, or the content within this book, without the consent of the author or publisher.

Disclaimer Notice:

Please note the information contained within this document is for educational and entertainment purposes only. All effort has been executed to present accurate, up to date, reliable, complete information. No warranties of any kind are declared or implied. Readers acknowledge that the author is not engaged in the rendering of legal, financial, medical or professional advice. The content within this book has been derived from various sources. Please consult a licensed professional before attempting any techniques outlined in this book.

By reading this document, the reader agrees that under no circumstances is the author responsible for any losses, direct or indirect, that are incurred as a result of the use of the information contained within this document, including, but not limited to, errors, omissions, or inaccuracies.

YOUR FREE GIFT!

Thinking, "Why a logbook for mushroom cultivation?" Precision is key! Every detail is vital, and a checklist ensures nothing slips through the cracks, guiding you to a fruitful harvest.

Ready for a thriving mushroom garden? Click the link below. This isn't just a list—it's a pathway to abundant, quality mushrooms, covering everything from strain selection and substrate preparation to optimal growing conditions and harvest.

Step into efficient mushroom cultivation—your abundant harvest awaits!

Scan the QR Code Below to Download The Logbook

TABLE OF CONTENTS

INTRODUCTION

There are few activities in this life that are as satisfying as growing your own food, and of the many foods you could grow, mushrooms are perhaps the most fascinating and versatile organisms you can find. However, with this versatility, there's bound to be a learning curve—that's why "mycology," or the study of fungi, and the ensuing cultivation of mushrooms is recognized as entirely different from other forms of agriculture. It takes a deep knowledge and a variety of skills to be proficient in cultivating mushrooms—but with time and due diligence, I believe it can be as simple a task as baking a cake. That confidence is exactly what this book sets out to develop within you. Any process, when understood in detail, can be learned by someone who was once a lay person. That's all-mushroom cultivation is—a process. So, leave any apprehension here, on the very first page, and let's set sail on an awe-inspiring adventure into the wonderful world of fungi, mycelium, and most importantly—mushrooms!

Welcome to the Wonderful World of Fungi

Fungi are more than mere organisms; they're a community, a culture, and, perhaps more importantly, a sacred commodity that has been celebrated in human life for thousands—if not millions—of years. Ancient civilizations worshipped mushrooms as if they were the closest thing to the gods that human life would ever know. However, this may only be the profundities of the "magic" variety—psilocybin mushrooms. As we explore just a few of the ever-increasing selections of edible mushrooms, you'll soon discover that all mushrooms are magic in their own right. From boosting the immune system and reducing inflammation, to improving cognition and possibly even preventing Alzheimer's, there's arguably a mushroom out there to treat any ailment or facilitate any improvement you wish to make. Yet, I don't think most people know the names of more than about five species of mushrooms, let alone how to grow them. This book seeks to correct this deficiency!

What you've stumbled on is one of the world's most powerful secrets, that was admittedly never a secret at all; you're standing at the doorway of the beautiful world of fungi, and I'd like to extend to you the warmest welcome! I know you will find the answers you are looking for in the material that follows, and I hope that by embracing the humble practice of mushroom cultivation your life is forever changed—for the better—just as mine has since my very first encounter with a spore print.

What Makes Mushrooms So Special?

Mushrooms, truffles, toadstools, and puffballs—what do these different fungus fruits have in common? They're all whistleblowers. To understand why mushrooms are unique, we first have to understand the underground network these above-ground organisms have allowed us to discover. Mushrooms and the other "fruiting bodies" grow from branches of fungi in the ground called hyphae. These branches make up part of a much more extensive, elaborate network of fungi known as mycelium. If you're a green thumb, you might equate this network of mycelium to the root networks that your plants make, but what makes mycelium so incredible is that it's likely invisible in your soil amongst those roots, and you probably have no idea.

So, this brings us to the question—what makes mushrooms unique? Well, if we consider mycelium to be the magical force that gives life to much of nature, then mushrooms are the agents that allow this force to spread and continue thriving. For mycelium's growth to occur, the soil we wish to grow in first has to be "inoculated," a term that you will be well acquainted with by the end of this book (if you aren't already). A spore—almost like a seed, but microscopic—needs to be present in the soil for inoculation to take place. The spores required for this to happen are located within a mushroom's gills, and every time the wind blows or a mushroom is pried or prodded, hundreds, even *thousands* of spores will drop onto the forest floor or become airborne. In doing this, they continue to inoculate our soil, maintaining the mycelium network and spreading it far and wide..

So, mycelium may be the force giving life to everything we see, but without mushrooms and other fruiting bodies, it would lose the ability to spread like wildfire to provide that life. This makes mushrooms a seminal part of all life on Earth—they are the frontline in the operation that turns waste matter into organic matter, thus making organic and human life possible. We simply wouldn't survive as a species on this planet we've come to know and love without them—and that's before we've even considered their nutritional properties!

What You Will Discover—In This Book and On Your Own

Let's be honest—not everyone is cut out to be a mycologist. In this book, we'll be breaking down a lot of the confusing terms used widely in the mushroom cultivation industry, translating them into plain English. That way, you won't feel as though you are out of your depth as a beginner. Sure, some aspects of growing mushrooms may seem complicated at first, but by gaining a deeper understanding of the practice, you will soon come to realize that growing mushrooms is a simple a step-by-step process. Luckily, this book will provide you with all the instructions you need, and we'll also be taking the time to understand why growing our own mushrooms can be so advantageous and enjoyable.

The next key discovery you will make is that you don't need a laboratory and a degree in Biology in order to successfully grow mushrooms—all of the guides and information in this book have been compiled with you, *the beginner,* in mind. That means we won't be using any special, hard-to-get equipment. We'll be focusing on growing mushrooms in your garden outside, as well as indoors, to ensure that no matter the amount of space you have, you have the opportunity to grow your own mushrooms. We will also be providing you with a number of step-by-step instructions on how to build the necessary equipment at low cost and with minimal technology.

Lastly, the book will cover 10 DIY projects that you can easily do at home with minimal tools. This will be for any equipment we may need to utilize when growing our mushrooms that may be expensive. Some will simply be tools that can be used to make the process easier for you, or allow you to achieve better results.

So, what are we waiting for? Let's learn how to grow mushrooms in our gardens, at home!

CHAPTER 1
Why Grow Your Own?

A t this point you might still be wondering whether growing your own mushrooms is something that would be worth your while. After all, there is a lot of work that goes into gathering the materials, learning the skills, and maintaining your mushroom patch. In this chapter I'd like to briefly list a few of the many and considerable advantages of growing your own mushrooms at home.

What Makes it Worth the Effort?

It is safe to say that growing mushrooms is a time-consuming hobby, which begs the question: Why do people bother doing it? Mushroom cultivation is becoming more and more popular, so there has to be a reason why people are willing to spend their time learning skills that were once limited to farmers and mycologists, right? This is not to say that mushroom cultivation is a full-time job; on the contrary, with the step-by-step instructions, tips and information presented in this book, you will learn to optimize the mushroom growing time to be worth the effort—without spending more than a few hours a week. I can guarantee you that the rewards of growing mushrooms far outweigh any challenges you may face in order to be successful. You'll soon understand why this practice has recently become so popular and what makes the effort worthwhile.

You Get to Enjoy Variety, While Staying Safe

By learning to grow your mushrooms, you can explore various flavor profiles and textures in your meals—without running the risk of eating a mushroom that you may not have yet correctly identified. Even if you'd like to forage your mushrooms at some point, by growing them at your own pace and getting familiar with their characteristics, you can ensure that you will be sufficiently well-informed to correctly identify specific species in the wild. So, in this sense, growing mushrooms has a sort of compounding effect on the quality of experiences: It will enable you to go out into the wilderness and explore, and enjoy a different cuisine—while keeping safe.

It's a Great Way to Save Money

Mushrooms, even just the grocery store varieties, are versatile ingredients in your cooking. From mushroom burgers to mushroom chips, these fungi can substitute a wide array of other foods with their flavor and texture that can change dramatically based on how you cook them. This versatility only expands when you start experimenting with more exotic species. Many of these mushrooms can stand on their own as well. So, what's my point?

Well, when you have such an abundance of versatile mushrooms at your disposal, suddenly you'll find you don't have to buy *nearly* as many ingredients from the grocery store. All of a sudden, you no longer need to take that extra steak or chicken fillet—because you have this new recipe with mushrooms that's just as appetizing and costs you far, far less! Hayden Lejuene (2020) estimates that oyster mushrooms can be bought for between $5 and $15 per pound and shiitake mushrooms for between $12 and $24 per pound. This of course depends on whether you buy your mushrooms wholesale or retail. By growing your own however, you can save around $40 dollars each month once your mushroom farm is up and running.

And a Great Way to Make Money

As mentioned above, growing your own mushrooms represents a number of great ways to save money. However, cultivating and harvesting your own mushrooms can also prove to be a very lucrative business venture. In the past few years, there has been an increase in demand for sustainable homegrown mushrooms. There are a variety of approaches to running a mushroom business, including medicinal mushrooms, meat alternatives, and ingredients for beauty products. All you truly need to create a booming mushroom-selling business is a passion for the fungi and a good business plan. Once you are ready, you can either sell your produce fresh at a market or dry the mushrooms and begin a local business.

You Get to Become More Self-Sufficient

Continuing on with our previous point, wouldn't it be great to know that if the grocery stores closed tomorrow due to a crisis, you'd have at least a few days of food to keep you going? When you grow your mushrooms (or produce in general), you won't have to rely on grocery stores, and you won't have to worry about food shortages. You are also guaranteed to have fresher mushrooms if you grow them yourself. Not only will you no longer have to travel to a grocery store to find they don't stock the mushroom variety you need, but becoming self-sufficient is also much better for the environment. There is no need to rely on using fossil fuel to as you drive from one store to the next. You can simply walk to your mushroom farm and gather the ones you need.

You Get to Learn a New Skill

Self-sufficiency goes hand-in-hand with self-reliance; both stem from the skills you learn when growing and tending to your mushrooms. While growing mushrooms is often seen as simple enough for anyone to understand, there is definitely a learning curve involved in cultivating mushrooms. Knowing how to identify, forage, and cultivate mushrooms is a very handy skill. Once you understand the basics and see yourself succeeding, you can educate others on mushroom growing as well. By increasing your mushroom yield, you will gain patience and responsibility, learn a new appreciation for nature, and expand on your creativity and sense of discovery. You will find that you gather many insights from experience—and you will find yourself growing as a human being alongside the mushrooms!

Getting Closer With Nature

Cultivating your mushrooms, gathering and harvesting them once they have matured, involves spending a great deal of time outside. As you find yourself working with your mushrooms, and perhaps foraging for others, you will grow closer to nature and foster a new appreciation for our beautiful world. Once you have successfully grown your mushrooms and have learned how to harvest and prepare them properly, you will find that you will begin to notice and appreciate other fungi, plants, and natural living beings. You will start to understand the life cycle of mushrooms and admire their resilience in the wild—this will spark your curiosity for other aspects of nature. Once you begin to work with something as fascinating as mushrooms and become more aware of the natural world's rhythms, you will find that you like to spend *more* time with nature.

You Get to Reap the Health Benefits

When you grow your own mushrooms, you don´t need to worry about the safety of the food you consume. Because you are involved in every step of the process, you can be confident that they were grown ethically and that no unnecessary chemicals were used. There is, of course, the bonus that homegrown mushrooms taste *far* better than store-bought. Taste aside however, mushrooms also possess many nutritional benefits. They are a rich, low-calorie source of fiber, antioxidants, and protein; they are an essential source of various B vitamins; and help maintain several bodily functions, like good eyesight and proper digestion. While mushrooms are a great source of protein, they should not act as a replacement for protein. According to Siddhi Camila Lama (2019), depending on the variety of mushrooms, they can only account for a maximum of 7% of your daily value for protein. Meat generally accounts for between 37% and 55% of your daily value, whereas other plant-based options like tofu or tempeh can account for between 8% and 50%. So, if you want to incorporate mushrooms into your diet as a source of protein, be sure to supplement the rest of your daily value with another source of protein.

It is an Essential Part of the Ecosystem

Mushroom cultivation offers many critical ecological benefits. While we might consider the part we eat, the fruiting body, to be the most crucial element of the mushroom, the network of mycelium is really the most essential. You can think of mycelium as the vegetative roots of your fungus or mushroom crops. Mycelium is a stringy, white material found in the soil of healthy forests. Where mycelium networks are found, they aid in purifying nearby water, breaking down any dangerous contaminants and increasing soil fertility. Fungi, mushrooms, and mycelium are an integral part of any ecosystem, and by growing your own, you contribute to the upkeep and flourishing of existing ecosystems. Mushrooms, and other fungi, act as natural decomposers and recyclers, breaking down organic matter, fertilizing the soil, and providing nutrients to other plants.

It is an Environmentally Friendly Practice

Mushrooms can be grown using a variety of substrates (material from which an organism lives, grows and obtains its nourishment), and some of these can be items you would otherwise discard or compost. Instead of disposing of materials like straw bales, coffee grounds or rotten logs, you can use these to grow mushrooms! It may seem more difficult than other growing techniques, but you will learn many new skills and recycle items that might have been damaging to the environment in some way. When growing your mushrooms, you could also become involved in "mycorestoration." This is the process of utilizing fungi to restore damaged and disturbed habitats and ecosystems. On the whole, working with mushrooms is a very sustainable practice that, when done on a small scale, has minimal impact on the surrounding environment.

Mushroom Growing is Fun and Educational

Though the advantages covered above are convincing enough to persuade even the *biggest* sceptic, another real benefit of growing your own mushrooms is that the entire process will be fun—and educational! Working with mushrooms—growing them, harvesting them, and foraging for species you have yet to discover—is incredibly entertaining. It can become a joyful and awe-inspiring hobby through which you meet many new, like-minded people. You will find that observing the process of growth and trying different techniques proves to be incredibly fun! Watching the mushrooms develop, you learn more about their life cycles and how they work in various ecosystems. Cultivating mushrooms can be the most fun, learning and working, that you have ever had.

As this chapter comes to an end, you have been introduced to a number of reasons why growing mushrooms is well worth your time. In the next chapter, we will introduce you to the ins and outs of an actual mushroom. So, let's explore this wonderful fungus even further!

CHAPTER 2
What is a Mushroom?

While most people, whether they have worked with mushrooms or not, would be able to point one out, or describe its basic shape and size, few laypeople *truly* know what a mushroom is. If you want to grow your own mushrooms and grow multiple varieties, you will have to be able to answer the question: "What is a mushroom?" Once you answer this question, you can begin asking others: "What role do mushrooms and fungi play in the ecosystem? How do fungi differ from other plants? Can fungi even be classified as a plant?" The answers to these questions contain valuable information you need to know before progressing. In this chapter I will present you with all of the answers to these questions, along with additional information that will aid you in your journey of cultivation.

The Ins and Outs of Mushrooms and Fungi

Now we are taking a more in-depth approach to learning about mushrooms and their quirks. It is important to remember that all mushrooms are fungi—but not all fungi are mushrooms. Fungi are eukaryotic organisms and can be classed as either single cell or complex multicellular organisms. Microorganisms like mold, yeast, and mushrooms are fungi. Mushrooms, along with some other fungi, are classified under the biological Kingdom: fungi. The organisms in this classification are often referred to as "heterotrophs." Fungi, like mushrooms, play an important role in the ecosystem. However, in order to explore their importance further, one must first be able to identify mushrooms.

What is a Mushroom?

If you are new to mycology, you might not know that a mushroom has two main parts: the mycelium network, which runs underground and can span acres; and the fruiting flower, often referred to as the sporophore, which is found aboveground. What we label as a "mushroom" is in reality only the fruit of a much larger fungus, and the mushroom is simply the reproductive structure that this fungus produces—it is the part of the larger fungus, which spreads spores. The fruiting body, i.e., the mushroom, has many different parts—all of which are important to know and understand in order to grow mushrooms properly.

Depending on the variety, the physical attributes of one mushroom type can differ significantly from another. Some mushrooms are difficult to spot in the wilderness as they expertly blend into their environment. Others are brightly colored and can be spotted quite easily; the *Amanita muscaria*, or fly agaric, is bright red with white spots and the variant most people associate with wild mushrooms. As many people know, some mushroom types are safe to eat and pose no harm to humans. However, there are a number of mushroom types that humans should never interact with, as they can cause serious harm. When growing mushrooms, you will not have to fret too much over the harmful types, as you will be working with those you know are safe for human consumption.

General Information About Mushrooms

In this section, I would like to offer you some general information and interesting facts about mushrooms. To succeed in cultivating the best mushrooms, knowing exactly what a mushroom is, and how they work, is essential. While this is certainly useful knowledge to possess as you begin cultivating mushrooms, this section is aimed at broadening your general understanding of the fungi—and piquing your curiosity even further!

The Kingdom fungi, to which mushrooms belong, houses an average of more than 144,000 known species, which includes various species of yeasts, molds, and rusts. There are about 10,000 different types of mushroom known to us, and while a large number of these are actually poisonous—so interacting with these ones should *always* be avoided, as even touching a small amount of spores can be harmful—some are useful to humans. Even though we generally classify those fit for consumption as "vegetables," mushrooms are separate from plants and animals, which is why they are classed as fungi.

We humans might like eating these fungi, but animals generally avoid them. To animals, they lack any substantial nutritional value, consist mostly of water, and are often extremely toxic. The mushrooms we eat are usually cultivated rather than grown and foraged for in the wild.

Mushrooms grow from the hidden part of the fungus, i.e., the part found underground—the mycelium. As we have seen, the mycelium is a complex network of fibers that can grow extremely large, often spanning several acres. In order to grow as it does, mycelium absorbs the nutrients it needs from decaying and dead organic matter. Mycelium plays an incredibly important role in our planet´s ecosystem: it secretes enzymes that aid in breaking down organic matter. This underground network not only links fungi together but also allows trees to communicate with one another.

Mycelium is an incredible organism; we need to carefully consider it when growing mushrooms. The goal of this organism is to reproduce and keep the species alive. If the conditions for reproduction aren't adequate, mycelium can remain hidden and dormant for many years. Once the conditions are perfect, mycelium produces the fruit (mushrooms), which then produces and disperses spores.

You will work with mycelium to properly grow and nurture your chosen mushrooms. Due to its importance, working with this organism might seem a bit daunting, but I can reassure you that the step-by-step guidance in this book will ensure that you succeed in taming mycelium—and growing the perfect mushrooms.

The Role of Fungi in the Ecosystem

I have already alluded to the importance of fungi in the ecosystem, as knowing how fungi interact with their surroundings is crucial knowledge when properly cultivating mushrooms. In energy cycling between and within ecosystems, fungi hold an important role. They can be found in freshwater, marine, and terrestrial environments. Fungi are a sundry community of decomposers, and include bacteria, small invertebrates, and larger invertebrates. So, let's explore the role of fungi in an ecosystem in a bit more detail.

The food cycle would be incomplete without organisms like fungi that are natural recyclers and decomposers. Certain elements are scarce in the natural environment, but biological systems need some in abundance. Through their metabolic activity, fungi aid in releasing the much-needed elements from decaying matter, making them available for other living organisms. Due to their mode of nutrition, fungi are able to break down insoluble and large molecules.

Despite our understanding of fungi as something that rots our food or causes diseases, fungi play an important role in human life. Their part in the nutrient cycle in ecosystems influences the well-being of humans on a large scale. Nutrient cycling refers to how nutrients move from decomposers to soil and are then absorbed by plants. Nutrients are essential for plant growth, but are not always freely accessible or available through water and soil. Decomposers, like mushrooms, transform nutrients and make them available to plants, breaking down organic matter thereby increasing the nutrient availability in the soil and allowing plants to absorb the necessary nutrients through their roots.

Fungi are part of crucial mutualistic relationships that greatly benefit the ecosystem. A mutualistic relationship refers to a symbiotic relationship that benefits both parties involved. Fungi form mutualistic relationships with various organisms, including animals, algae, cyanobacteria and plants. These mutualistic relationships display one of the roles fungi play in the ecosystem. A good model of a mutualistic relationship is fungus–plant mutualism. This mutualism consists of the establishment of mycorrhizae— the association between fungi and plants. The term mycorrhiza refers to the role of the fungus in the plant´s rhizosphere, or root system. Between 80% and 90% of plant species have a mycorrhizal partner, and both plants and fungi benefit from this partnership.

In the ecosystem, fungi fall at the end of the food chain. Alongside other decomposers, fungi complete the cycle. As they break down organic matter from dead plants and animals, and return the nutrients to the soil, the current cycle ends and a new one can begin.

Are Mushrooms Plants?

Although many argue that anything that grows naturally or organically is a plant, fungi are in a separate scientific category, thereby firmly solidifying their non-plant status. Mushrooms are a fungus type with a plant-like form, as mushrooms have stems, caps, and cell walls. In what ways, then, do fungi like mushrooms, differ from plants?

A mushroom's life cycle begins underground as a type of white fluff, most commonly referred to as mycelium. As outlined earlier, mycelium is the fungal thread from which mushrooms sprout. When circumstances are conducive to growth, food is present and the temperature and humidity are at the proper levels, buds will form underground and seek out sunlight. These are the fruit of the mycelium we have come to know as mushrooms. At first, the fruit is a small, usually white ball that will eventually grow to be a mushroom. Once mature, the cap will open and release millions of spores. The wind spreads the spores and, once they have made contact with the ground again, form another mycelium network.

One of the main characteristics of plants is that they contain chlorophyll, which is used to convert energy gathered from sunlight into carbohydrates. Mushrooms *do not* contain chlorophyll and therefore do not photosynthesize, so the carbohydrates they need are taken from other plants, usually in a mutualistic relationship.

Both plants and mushrooms have cell walls, but the compositions of these differ greatly. A plant's cell walls are composed of cellulose, while a mushroom's cell walls are generated from complex polysaccharides called chitin and glucan. The way in which a mushroom's cell walls are composed enhances its structural integrity and aids in protecting it from predators.

Mushroom Parts and How They Interact With One Another

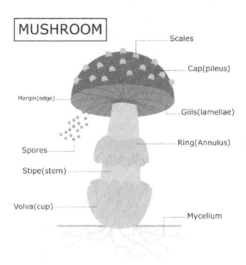

As with all living organisms, there are several parts, and with a mushroom, each part interacts with the others to reproduce and keep the fungi healthy and alive. It is important to have detailed knowledge of the parts of a mushroom in order to properly forage for them, or grow your own. Being able to identify each part and its function will allow you to differentiate between edible and poisonous mushrooms, and aid in your understanding of the mushroom life cycle and their reproduction methods. In this section, we'll take an in-depth look at the different parts of mushrooms and how they interact.

A mushroom has two principal parts: the mycelium and the fruiting body, which consists of a number of different structures. Of these two parts, mycelium is viewed as the main part of the entire organism and is what allows the mushroom to form and grow. As we have seen, the mycelium is the part of the fungus that forms underground, and which we rarely see. The mycelium network is vast and complex and consists of cells that form thin fibers, not unlike the roots of plants. These fibers grow and spread underneath the ground, searching for and absorbing nutrients. Mycelium forms through the spreading of mushroom spores. Once the spore finds a location with conditions suitable for growth, it will germinate. During the germination process, it produces hyphae, thread-like filaments that grow and connect to form the mycelium network. The majority of the fungus is the underground mycelium, while the mushroom is simply the product of its need to reproduce.

The fruiting body is the umbrella-shaped structure of the mushroom that many presume to be the main, (and only), part of the fungus. The fruit, or sporophore, is the fleshy part of the fungus and can either be poisonous or edible. It can either grow above ground or on a suitable surface, provided the conditions are conducive to growth, and its objective is to produce and distribute spores. This fruiting body possesses a number of different structures, (see image above) and, depending on the type of mushroom, some of the structures may not be present. Most mushrooms have a cap, gills, a stem, spores, a volva, hyphae, and mycelium. Some of these structures, like mycelium, are present in all mushrooms as they are crucial to survival. There is undoubtedly more to mushrooms than simply a stem and an umbrella-shaped cap. In the following section, we'll look more closely at the different structures that make up the part of the fungus we refer to as: a mushroom.

The Mushroom Cap

Technically, one would refer to the mushroom cap as a "pileus," and mushrooms with a cap-like structure are "pileate." This is the uppermost, umbrella-shaped part of a mushroom. The cap can be either cone-shaped, flat, or spherical-shaped, and grows in various colors and textures. Mushroom caps can differ in texture and color for a variety of reasons, mainly due to the mushroom's stage of development and its species. As the mushroom develops, the shape of the cap will change as it grows and matures. The surface that produces spores is contained in the cap and consists of pores, teeth, or gills. The purpose of the cap is to protect the surface on which the spores are produced. You can imagine it works much the same way an umbrella does—the shape of the umbrella shields you from the weather and similarly the shape of the cap protects the spore-producing surface.

The Gills

When observing the area underneath the cap, you will see thin, almost paper-like shapes that are layered closely together. Like the mushroom cap, gills can be various colors and have marked features that you can use to identify different species. The color of the gills, their shape, and the distance between each structure all play a role in their identification. The place and the manner in which they attach to the mushroom stem will also help you identify the species. However, some mushroom species do not have gills. Instead, these species, like porcinis, might have pores which are minuscule, tightly packed tubes that bear a resemblance to a sponge. A species like lion's mane has needles or teeth in place of gills. The purpose of gills, or lamellae, is to create and spread as many spores as possible.

The Spores

Though invisible without a microscope, mushroom spores are incredibly important structures in the body of the fungus. Produced in the gills, spores are minute, unicellular reproductive cells. In terms of color, spores tend to be some shade of black, brown, pink or white, although some species have green, orange, and yellow spores. Mycologists often use the color, shape, and size of the spore to identify the species of fungi.

Essentially, the spore is a seed that houses the genetic material needed to grow new networks of mycelium which will, in turn, produce new mushrooms. Spores are released at the end of the growth cycle and are distributed by animals, humans, water, and wind. To germinate, spores need to settle in an area that is moist, shaded, and warm.

A Ring

Some mushroom stems have a ring of tissue wrapped around them. This is the residual part of a partial veil, a thin material that provides additional protection for the gills when the mushroom is still young. The partial veil is attached to the cap when the mushroom is immature, but as the cap grows and the mushroom matures, the veil breaks and exposes the gills. Often, the remains of the partial veil will form a ring around the stem. As with other structures of the mushroom, the ring can be used to identify and classify the mushroom. The type of ring—whether thin and stringy, or prominent and thick—as well as the shape and position of the ring, can be used to identify the mushroom.

The Stem

The stem, also known as the stipe, elevates the cap above the ground and acts as its support structure. The stem's purpose is to aid in scattering the spores. As many mushrooms use animals or the wind to spread their spores, the cap and gills need to be elevated above the ground to ensure the spores are released into the wind or are able to latch onto passing animals. The attributes of the stem, like texture, shape, and size, all aid in identifying the mushroom type. Certain mushroom varieties do not have a stem at all, and others have gills that grow down the stem. Mushrooms that do have stems are called "stipitate".

The Volva

This structure, also referred to as the universal layer, is a tissue that aids in protecting the young mushroom of certain species as they grow. The volva is located at the base of the mature mushroom's stem, and is often seen in species that grow from the ground. As the mushroom grows, it breaks through the veil and leaves this bottom part at its base. The thin tissue left over forms a cup-like shape at the base and is crucial to identifying mushrooms in the wild. It is a significant feature in many poisonous mushrooms.

The Mycelium

At this point, you should be familiar with the mycelium, which is a network of long hyphae fibers, the color of which can oscillate between cream and white. Mycelium is the vegetative, non-reproductive structure of the mushroom that grows in organic matter or soil. Its purpose is to expand the area from which the fungi can gather nutrients. The network grows outwards as it looks for nutrients and water, and transports those needed to the mushroom to aid in its growth, allowing it to release spores.

The Hyphae

The network of mycelium is made up of hyphae, which are miniscule, thread-like filaments that connect and grow to form the mycelium. The hyphae's aim is to absorb nutrients from its environment and deliver these to the other parts of the fungus.

As you can see, all parts of the fruiting body aid in spreading spores and reproducing in order to create more fungi. All of these structures are dependent on the hyphae and mycelium for nutrients and growth. The structures of the fruiting body are crucial to mushroom identification and classification. As you begin to grow your own, you will be able to spot the differences easily and identify mushrooms based on the characteristics of their structures, or the lack of certain parts. As your mushrooms grow, you will see that most of these parts are crucial to their reproduction and survival.

Mushroom Classification

Mushrooms can be divided into three broad classes: mycorrhizae, parasites, and saprotrophs. The different species of mushrooms can be placed into one of these three categories based on how they function, their purpose, their relationship with nature, and so on. Let's look at each of the three classes of mushroom:

Mycorrhizal Mushrooms

Mushrooms in this class establish a symbiotic relationship with the roots of live trees. This symbiotic relationship is a mutualistic one in some ways, as the mushrooms take nutrients from the trees. In exchange, the trees get some nutrients back and the fungi aid in creating a larger, healthier root system. These fungi use the mycelium network to interact with plant and tree roots. Both main types of mycorrhizal fungi, ectomycorrhizae and endomycorrhizae, form mushrooms—though not all of these are edible. Mushrooms play a critical role in the ecosystems of forests. You will find chanterelles, porcini mushrooms and truffles under this classification.

Parasitic Mushrooms

This mushroom category settles down on living trees without any mutualistic relationship. Instead, they draw nutrients from the tree until it can no longer survive. This makes it a symbiotic relationship in which only one party benefits and the host (the tree) is harmed. Parasitic mushrooms receive all their nutrients from decomposed organic material but systematically drain the life of living organisms instead of waiting for the organism to die. The honey mushroom is an example of a parasitic mushroom that could manifest under the right conditions.

Saprophytic Mushrooms

Most fungi are saprophytic, which are entirely harmless and sometimes beneficial. The mushrooms in this category live on the organic matter of dead trees after they have been killed by parasitic mushrooms, and feed on other organic matter like fallen leaves and plant roots. Unlike parasitic mushrooms, these do not need a live host and prefer to feed on dead animal and plant remains. These mushrooms can be very beneficial in breaking down organic matter and making it available for plants. Saprophytic mushrooms pull nutrients, minerals, and carbon dioxide from the organic matter. Examples of mushrooms from this classification include oyster mushrooms and shiitake.

Further classifications of mushrooms that should also be considered are gourmet, medicinal, psychoactive, and poisonous mushrooms. In this book, we'll only be working with gourmet and medicinal mushrooms, and you will find that the types of mushrooms in these categories can often be found in both. The properties and ways in which to identify psilocybin and poisonous mushrooms will not be covered here.

Gourmet Mushrooms

This mushroom category contains dried or fresh mushrooms that are rich and full of flavor, often used in gourmet foods. In all likelihood, gourmet mushrooms are not the kind of mushrooms you would find in your local grocery store. Gourmet mushrooms are far more expensive and often rarer than the mushrooms we are used to buying. Some of these mushrooms can only grow under specific conditions or in certain parts of the world. Gourmet mushrooms can be foraged from the wild or cultivated; some chefs choose to cultivate their own while others prefer foraging for their gourmet mushrooms. Examples of gourmet mushrooms include morel mushrooms, truffles, and scotch bonnet mushrooms.

Medicinal Mushrooms

Medicinal mushrooms are macroscopic fungi used as powder or extracts to alleviate, heal or prevent certain diseases, and as part of a balanced diet. Mushrooms have been used for medicinal purposes for centuries and have a rich and fascinating history. Only recently has modern medicine fully accepted the benefits of using medicinal mushrooms and begun embracing them in healing practices. Medicinal mushrooms were part of traditional medicine for many centuries, providing immune support, a source of antioxidants, help with inflammation, balance to blood sugar, supporting brain, cognition and nervous system support and increasing stamina and energy.

Psychoactive Mushrooms

You might be more familiar with some of the other names for this classification, which includes names like "shrooms" and "magic mushrooms." These are mushrooms that occur naturally and are taken for their hallucinogenic effects. The most famous species of psychoactive mushrooms are the psilocybin mushrooms. Psilocybin mushrooms are psychedelic, meaning once ingested, they will affect all of your senses and alter your thinking, emotions, and sense of time. Psilocybin is the main ingredient in magic mushrooms and is converted into psilocin once consumed, a chemical with psychoactive properties. Psilocybin mushrooms are reported to have some medicinal benefits as well, when taken in small doses. They are currently in the final phases of research and testing to treat a variety of conditions including anxiety, depression, and inflammation.

Poisonous Mushrooms

You might have heard mushroom enthusiasts say "All mushrooms are edible, but some you only get to eat once!" Not all poisonous mushrooms will result in death for humans or animals. Some do damage to your organs or release toxins that cause harm when they are touched. When cultivating mushrooms, it is important to be sure you aren't growing a poisonous species, as some harmful mushrooms tend to disguise themselves as harmless fungi. It is worth noting that no seller would ever stock or sell poisonous mushrooms, so when growing your own mushrooms, it is impossible to grow poisonous mushrooms. The only way to obtain poisonous mushrooms is by foraging for them.

In this book, we will not look at poisonous or psilocybin mushrooms in more detail. Instead, I will focus on teaching you about gourmet and medicinal mushrooms, as these are some of the more common ones you will want to grow. In the next chapter we'll take a closer look at some of the best places you can grow mushrooms at home, and under what conditions mushrooms need to be grown.

CHAPTER 3
Where to Grow Mushrooms

When you are growing your own mushrooms, especially at home where you might not have acres of space available, it is important to consider where you can grow your mushrooms. Deciding on a location will depend on a variety of factors including space, climate, the variety of mushrooms you want to grow, and so on. Mushrooms need to be grown under very specific circumstances and that is what I will be discussing in this chapter. We'll look at the perfect mushroom growing conditions and discuss the benefits of growing mushrooms both indoors and outdoors.

Where can Mushrooms be Grown?

As I have mentioned, you can grow your own mushrooms both indoors and outdoors. However, not all mushrooms can be grown indoors as you cannot always replicate the exact environment they need to grow properly. You can successfully grow a few mushroom varieties indoors, and they often thrive in an indoor environment as this tends to be a more controlled area where the proper growing conditions can be consistently maintained. Other mushrooms, like shiitake, are better grown outside on substrates like logs or stumps in an environment that more closely reflects their natural environment.

Of course, nature makes the mushroom cultivation process look easy, but if you cannot maintain high humidity levels or provide adequate fresh air, the process can be very tricky. Certain things outside your control will influence the growing process, but with the help of this book, the proper conditions can be created and maintained, and you will be one step closer to growing healthy, thriving mushrooms.

When cultivating mushrooms at home, it is essential to be knowledgeable about the ideal mushroom-growing climate. Mushrooms prefer dark, warm, humid, and moist growing conditions. Creating and maintaining these conditions might seem simple, but there are specifications that need to be fulfilled to create the ideal climate. In the following section, we'll take a more in-depth look at the various growing conditions and their requirements.

Humidity

During various stages of the growing phase, the humidity level will need to be altered to accommodate the fungi and ensure proper growth. Humidity aids in creating the optimal amount of moisture required by the fungi to flourish. The humidity level will vary from species to species as some are perfectly content growing in low humidity while other mushrooms require high humidity. You will need to get the combination of humidity and other requirements just right to see your mushrooms grow properly. Luckily, this book will guide you through everything step-by-step.

During the fruiting phase, when you will finally be able to see your mushrooms form and grow, maintaining the right amount of humidity is incredibly important. For sufficient growing conditions, you will need to mimic the natural environment in which the chosen mushrooms grow as close as possible. Humidity and moisture go hand-in-hand in the growing process, and both are vital to growth in the surrounding environment and the substrate. Depending on the mushroom variety, the humidity levels need to fall somewhere between 70% and 100%. For example, during the fruiting stage of oyster mushrooms, the humidity levels should be between 80% and 95% for optimal growth. When mushrooms are pinning, high humidity is often extremely important as you do not want the baby mushroom pins to dry out and cease growing.

There are a number of ways in which you can maintain high humidity if the climate in which you live is not naturally humid. Still, even then you will need to be able to increase and decrease the humidity levels as the growing phases change. If the location allows, you can maintain high humidity by misting your mushrooms with water at least twice daily. However, if you live in a dry, hot climate you will need to utilize a humidity tent, which you can make using a plastic bag to maintain the prime humidity levels. Alternatively, you can opt to use a fruiting chamber, which will automate the entire process. A humidifier is linked to a humidity regulator thereby ensuring the levels remain correct throughout the fruiting phase. Mushrooms, like many other fungi, enjoy warm, humid conditions. However, this means contamination is likely to occur, but maintaining the correct level range of humidity and using quality materials can combat any contamination. In upcoming chapters, I offer you a guide on building the most widely used fruiting chambers, and creating and maintaining a sterile environment to avoid contamination in the growing environment.

Light

As with humidity levels, you will have to adjust the light levels the mushrooms experience during the various growing phases. Overall, mushrooms prefer little to no light, which means you will only need to make a few adjustments as the life cycle progresses. During incubation, it is best to keep your mushrooms in the dark areas as this mimics the natural conditions in which they will begin to grow. The growing area does not need to be in complete darkness; it simply needs to be a very low-light area like a dark room or cupboard. In contrast, you will want to utilize indirect light during the fruiting phase of the mushroom. Mycelium does not need light to grow in the substrate, however some varieties require light to set off mushroom production. When growing naturally, the mycelium uses sunlight to indicate that it is near the surface and can begin producing mushrooms. Placing your mushrooms in a spot with indirect natural light will help emulate these conditions.

Because mushrooms do not gain nutrients from sunlight in the same manner plants do, they do not need light to feed themselves and grow. That said, mushrooms need not be grown in a pitch-black environment. The darkness helps to preserve the moisture that spores require to reproduce. Common mushrooms can be grown in a basement as this ought to provide the ideal conditions, while mushrooms grown on logs for example, need to be kept away from direct sunlight as this can alter the temperature too much and dry the mushrooms out.

As alluded to already, little amounts of light do not harm mushrooms or stunt their growth. In fact, they do need some dim light to form the fruit, but you will only need to provide them with a few hours of light each day. If you are growing your mushrooms indoors, you can use a fluorescent lamp or keep them in an area with indirect sunlight to mimic their natural conditions. Light can, however, affect the temperature of the growing area, so it is best to use minimal light when the fruiting body is forming and maturing. When growing mushrooms outside, it is particularly important to ensure they are not exposed to too much light.

The amount of light the fungi need will depend on the species of mushroom you are growing. Some thrive in the sunlight, like the King Stropharia, and are ideal mushrooms to grow outdoors. The color of certain mushroom types is also affected by light levels, and you might find that the same species can look different when grown indoors than when grown outdoors.

Moisture

An adequate level of moisture is essential to mushroom growth. Without it, the mushrooms will dry out, which stunts their growth and eventually makes them unviable. The mycelium, and by extension the mushroom, receives most of its moisture from the substrate or growing medium, a moist, organic material that provides nutrients and energy. The type of substrate used will depend on the type of mushroom you are growing as different species prefer different substrates.

Like all fungi, mushrooms flourish when their growing environment is moist, and also like fungi, different mushroom types require different amounts of moisture; shiitake mushrooms grown on logs require a moisture level between 35% and 45% which involves soaking the logs for 48 hours, while button mushrooms need a moist growing medium like compost. This being said, mushrooms should be moist most of the time, but never wet. If you keep your mushrooms or substrate wet, you will never see proper growth and might end up only destroying all your fungi. You can mist your mushroom crop in intervals that work for you and the fungi to help them stay moist while keeping the substrate from getting too wet. Alternatively, you could also cover the container they are grown in with a damp cloth to aid in trapping the moisture.

Because mushrooms have no skin, they can easily lose the moisture necessary for their growth. Moisture is what helps the fungi produce its fruit, so if your mycelium and substrate do not contain the right amount of moisture, your mushrooms will never grow. Cultivating your mushrooms in a high-humidity environment will aid in retaining moisture and minimize water loss. When growing in the wild, mushrooms tend to disappear when the weather is exceedingly hot and dry, but often reappear when the humidity and moisture levels allow for a conducive growing environment. If you grow your mushrooms outdoors, you might see this happen, but you can combat it by keeping your mushrooms and the substrate moist, and shielding your crops from too much light, which can cause the water to evaporate.

Temperature

The temperature of the growing environment is the final characteristic of an ideal growing environment we will be discussing. Like the aspects mentioned in the previous sections, the climate's temperature will have to be adjusted as the fungi move through the various growing phases. The temperature is much easier to control when growing mushrooms indoors compared to growing mushrooms outdoors. However, as we will cover later, some mushrooms can comfortably grow outdoors and survive the changing temperatures. As with the previous sections, the type of mushroom will affect the temperature requirements during their life cycle.

Some mushrooms can tolerate more heat than others, and have a broader range of temperatures in which they can grow. Temperature affects the speed with which the mycelium can colonize the substrate. In the colonization phase, lower temperatures can slow the process down, while higher temperatures can speed up the process but also cause contamination. The requirements of the species of mushroom will determine the optimal temperature for them to grow. Oyster mushrooms for example thrive best in room temperature conditions during the colonization stage. As the temperature needs to change over the course of the life cycle, you might find it advantageous to use a fruiting chamber, especially when growing mushrooms indoors, that will help you regulate the temperature. You may also find that fans or heaters can help you create the ideal controller environments if you do not want to use a fruiting chamber.

Air that is too dry or an environment with extreme, fluctuating temperatures can easily harm or kill your mushrooms. Ideally, you want to keep your mushroom spawns warm to start the growing process properly. Once started, each phase generally requires the temperature to be lowered, which you can achieve with fans, fruiting chambers, or by moving your mushrooms to a cool, dark place. Wild mushrooms are less particular about the heat, however those cultivated at home will require special attention. Generally, homegrown mushrooms favor temperatures of 55-60°F; higher than 60°F might harm your crops.

Before you begin to finalize a location for your mushroom farm, it is important to check the area's temperature to ensure it will be conducive to growth. It is best to work with the average temperature guideline outlined above and move the individual species to cooler or warmer places as needed. Of course, you should constantly keep in mind that the required temperature will differ from one mushroom species to another. As we go through the step-by-step process of mushroom cultivation, the temperatures needed for various mushrooms will be provided to you.

Indoor Versus Outdoor Growing

As established, mushrooms can be grown both indoors and outdoors. Some species thrive indoors while others much prefer growing in an outdoor space and there are a number of benefits to both. In this section, we will take a brief look at some of the benefits of both, after which you can decide which will better suit your space and your needs.

Growing Mushrooms Indoors

There are several different mushroom varieties that you can grow indoors such as oyster and button mushrooms. While you would need to be very careful to maintain the ideal climate when growing mushrooms indoors, there are many great advantages to creating a small indoor mushroom farm.

- Indoor cultivation allows for a controlled growing environment.
- Mushrooms reach and complete the fruiting stage much quicker when grown indoors.
- Mushrooms can be grown year-round.
- Indoor cultivation can be achieved without soil, which allows for material, like coffee grounds, to be recycled.
- More mushroom species can reliably be grown when you can closely monitor and maintain the ideal environment.
- The systems used can be adapted to work in any space, thereby making them more accessible.

Growing Mushrooms Outdoors

Should it be more convenient to you and you have the space, mushrooms can also be grown outdoors. As with indoor cultivation, growing mushrooms outdoors also has a number of advantages.

- You are able to grow a larger quantity of mushroom as you have more space available.
- Outdoor conditions more closely relate to those mushrooms encountered when growing in the wild.
- You do not need to control and maintain the climate as closely in order to create the ideal environment.
- Outdoor cultivation allows you to grow a variety of different mushroom species and ensures you grow species that suit your needs.

As this chapter comes to a close, you can now narrow down the location in which you would like to grow your mushrooms. You can begin testing and checking the various areas, eliminating those that do not fit the requirements and will not contribute to the ideal growing climate. In the next chapter, I will guide you through an in-depth description of the life cycle of a mushroom and you will be one step closer to cultivating your own.

CHAPTER 4

The Life Cycle of a Mushroom

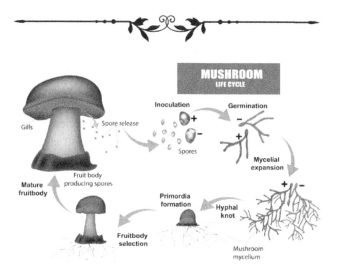

All living organisms, fungi included, go through a life cycle during which they are born, mature, and set out to reproduce in order to keep their species alive. In this chapter, you will be familiarized with each phase of a mushroom's lifecycle. It is crucial to take note of the different phases and how the fungi behave during each, as this is what you will need to monitor in order to harvest the mushrooms as soon as they are mature.

Dissemination on Spores

You can view the spores as the seed of the mushroom or of the fungi network as a whole. They are microscopic reproductive elements produced by mushrooms. The dispersal of spores both begins and ends the mushrooms' life cycle. The purpose of a mushroom is to release its spores in order to reproduce. Once the spores have been released, the mushroom has fulfilled its purpose and a mature mushroom will decompose shortly after the spores have been released. When moving, the spores might land near the parent fungi, but it is more likely that the spore will land farther away.

The scattering of spores is also the start of the life cycle for a new generation of mushrooms. The spores are released from the gills, which are situated underneath the mushroom cap. One single mushroom can produce hundreds of thousands of spores. Animals, wind and water aid in scattering the spores once they have been released and the spores. Once the spores have landed in an area with the ideal conditions, they begin germinating and will eventually produce both a mature mycelium network and a mature mushroom. This process is also known as inoculation, during which the spores find an appropriate substrate and if the conditions are favorable, the spores will begin germinating.

Once the spore has germinated, it will divide through mitosis and create a thread-like fiber—the hyphae—that will eventually branch out from the spore to form the mycelium network. Mycelium makes up the hyphae and is the main body of the fruiting mushroom. The hyphae create a tangled mass of threads, stretch over the environment within reach of the mycelium, and release chemicals that dissolve the food needed for growth and survival. The nutrients from the food are then digested and absorbed by the mushroom, though this process takes place further into the lifecycle of the fungi.

Growing into Hyphae

The hyphae are the basic fungal unit that contains the cytoplasm and genetic material of the mushroom. Mushroom spores are able to ascertain whether they have landed somewhere with an adequate growing environment. Once it has landed in the ideal environment, the spore will germinate and form a germ tube. This is the first multicellular outgrowth formed by a single-celled spore. Once this has formed, the process of differentiation and growth by means of mitosis begins. Once the spores start dividing they produce hyphae, which immediately set out to look for food and water.

Eventually, the germ tube will grow into hyphae (i.e. the structure used by fungi to gather nutrients and energy), and expand through the area. The thin, long strings of hyphae extend through the substrate, releasing digestive enzymes that break down organic matter to fuel the fungi's growth. The hyphae are groups of the same mushroom spore, and provided they are compatible, when the hyphae of one spore reaches another, they meet and combine, so beginning the process of mycelium formation.

Mushrooms technically cannot be divided into sexes and therefore there are no male or female spores. Instead, mushrooms have positive and negative mating types. There are no visible differences between positive and negative hyphae, but for reproduction to take place, the presence of the opposite type is necessary. The resulting new cell has two nuclei, which divides into new cells that also have two nuclei. The main aim of a hypha is to find a spore of the opposite type to bond with. The hypha extends until it meets a match and, when the opposite type of the same species is found, the hyphae bond and combine to create a new cell. If the hyphae are compatible, they "mate" and form fertile mycelium.

Mycelial Expansion

This is the phase during the life cycle in which we begin to see the growth process, and up until this point the process has largely taken place underground. The large colony or organized group that hyphae form is what we refer to as mycelium. The vast mycelium network that plays a critical role in the ecosystem is made up of various hyphae colonies. When compatible hyphae connect, it forms this functioning, fertile network of cells that becomes a single-celled organism that becomes the epicenter of a mushroom's life cycle and the natural ecosystem.

As it grows, mycelium extends and consumes the organic material found in the specific substrate the fungi thrive in. When mycelium has matured and is exposed to particular conditions, like the proper temperature and humidity levels, it will begin to fruit and produce mushrooms. The mushroom is fed nutrients through the mycelium, and once it has matured, it will release spores, and the life cycle begins again.

You could view mycelium as the root-like system of the mushroom, much like plant roots. The mycelium system remains rooted to the ground and substrate but can branch out and span several acres. Mycelium creates an environment that offers stability and nutrition to the fungi, allowing them to produce mushrooms. During this cycle phase, the mycelium finds and breaks down nutrients that the mushroom and the mycelium can use to fuel augmented growth. The mycelium acts as the immune system of the mushroom and aids in warding off competing and predatory organisms using various protective enzymes and compounds.

Mycelium breaks down dead organic matter and absorbs the remaining nutrients as it develops. This aids in mycelial expansion, which occurs exponentially throughout this stage. Within the mycelium, you will find all the nutrients needed for a mushroom to progress in its life cycle. From the growth of the mycelial network, we see hyphal knots form, from which the mushrooms we want to utilize will grow.

Hyphal Knots and Primordia

When the climate is ideal, the mycelium has returned and is ready to begin producing mushrooms, and structures called hyphal knots will begin to form. During this stage, the mycelium joins together to form a knot near the surface of the substrate of the soil. The process in which hyphal knots, or primordium, are formed is referred to as "pinning." These are the first visible indication that mushrooms will eventually form. The hyphal knot is the point at which the tiny pinhead and body of the mushroom begin to bud, but does not yet take form. The transformation from hyphal knots to pinheads (baby mushrooms) is the first visible process in the life cycle.

The mycelium begins to fruit either when all of the nutrients in the surrounding area have been absorbed or a change in the environment has transpired. To create the fruit, myriad enzymes are constructed around the hyphal knot. This creates a small white shape—the primordium—which is often called a tiny pinhead because it resembles a small mushroom cap. The remainder of the cycle is completely visible, as the primordia continue to grow until they have reached the size and shape of matured mushrooms.

From Small Pinhead to Mature Mushroom

The hyphal knots grow rather rapidly once they have formed and will eventually grow to become the mature mushrooms you can harvest. As you watch the primordia grow into fully shaped mushrooms, you will notice that most of the pinheads from the mycelium colony will stop growing. You can easily spot the healthy ones as they continue to sprout into mushrooms. The entire organism cleverly identifies the primordia with the most potential to survive and funnels nutrients to the selected ones to aid them in maturing into a fruiting body.

Simply put, most people view the mushroom as only the cap or the stem, which is only a small part of an entire fungal network. The mushroom only exists for a few days before it disappears. During this time the mushroom devotes all of its nutrients and energy towards advancing the fruiting bodies to allow spores to be released and dispersed. Generating spores forms the sexual reproduction phase of the life cycle. In this phase the mushroom is fully grown and ready to be harvested for culinary or medicinal use. As you know from Chapter two, the mushroom generally consists of a cap, gills, and a stem; during this final stage of the life cycle, the spores existing within the gills are released and spread in preparation for a new life cycle to begin. Once the fruit is ready the spores are released for propagation, and should they land on the appropriate substrate, they can germinate and create wonderful, new mushrooms.

Regardless of the growing process you follow or the scale on which you grow, the methods of the cultivation process will follow the same basic principles that all stem from a wild mushroom's life cycle. In the following section, I will briefly introduce you to the step-by-step process of cultivating mushrooms.

The Process of Mushroom Cultivation

This section will provide a brief overview of the main steps needed to cultivate mushrooms at home. The steps in the process will be covered more thoroughly in the next few chapters. Once the basics of mushroom cultivation have been covered, I will also provide you with the instructions for 10 DIY mushroom growing projects perfect for beginners where you can put theory into practice and gain direct experience with all of these steps. So, without further ado, let's get straight into the step-by-step process of mushroom cultivation.

Pick Your Mushroom

The first step to growing your own mushrooms is deciding which mushrooms you will cultivate. You will have to consider the needs you want to be fulfilled and choose your mushrooms based on which will most likely meet those needs. It is important to settle on specific mushroom strains as well, as each strain often has specific growing requirements.

Create a Sterile Environment

Before beginning, you need to create or select a sterile environment. A sterile environment will ensure no other fungi infiltrate the growing space and take nutrients for your mushrooms. Wild mushrooms do not grow in a sterile environment, however one is needed when growing mushrooms indoors as you are interested in maximizing the yield. You want to grow your mushrooms in a space that you can safely keep clean all the time, and that will stay clean all the time. Ensure that this space also has a clean surface on which you can keep your mushroom farm.

Choosing and Obtaining Mushroom Spawn

Mushroom spawn is any substance or substrate that has already been fully colonized by a mycelial network. You can obtain mushroom spawn in three ways: through a grow kit, by buying spawn from a supplier or farmer, or by growing your own. These options all have a variety of benefits and the type of mushroom you choose to grow will influence how you obtain the mushroom spawn.

Selection and Preparation of the Substrate

The substrate is any material that acts as a food source for the mycelium. Choosing a type of substrate, and preparing the substrate, will depend on the type of mushroom you are growing. Some species prefer a certain substrate while others will grow in any medium. Common substrates include coffee grounds, grain hulls, logs, straw, stumps, and woodchips.

Inoculation

This step is also referred to as germination. The spawn is brought into contact with the substrate in order to initiate growth and development. You need to move the mushroom spawn from the sterile container in which it was obtained, to the sterile substrate, which is in a sterile environment, for inoculation to begin. The sterile environment will give the spawn the best chance for growth and colonization.

Incubation

Incubation is also known as expansion or colonization. During this step the spawn needs time to grow throughout the substrate. This usually occurs a few days after inoculation. Depending on the type of substrate and mushroom, this step can take anywhere from 10 days to 36 months.

Inducing and Fruiting

As the environmental conditions change: usually the humidity levels and temperature, hyphal knots will begin to form and eventually shape into pinheads. These pins will draw nutrients and water from the substrate and begin to grow into mushrooms. During this step, you must closely observe the substrate and the mushrooms. The amount of fruit created and the color and texture of the mushrooms will tell you what they require. The four primary parameters you need to maintain and consider during this time include lighting, temperature, humidity, and oxygen levels.

Harvesting

It would be best to harvest at the right time when the cap margin is still curled but the gills are exposed. Provided you maintain the optimal climate, the substrate can produce a few flushes of mushrooms, allowing you to harvest mushrooms more than once. A flush refers to a crop of mushrooms. The harvesting time is short, usually only a few days. You want to harvest your mushrooms daily, as some mature sooner than others, to ensure you get the best quality fruit. Harvested mushrooms should be kept in a container that allows them to breathe, i.e., a container with some holes.

Storing Mushrooms and Preparing Them for Use

There are various ways your mushrooms can be stored, including freezing and drying your mushrooms. You can freeze your mushrooms if you would like to keep them for a longer time, although you will have to cook them before freezing or they will lose their texture. Once picked, wrap your mushrooms in a damp towel and keep them in a container that allows air circulation. Please do not wash your mushrooms before storing them as this can cause them to absorb too much moisture, making them soggy and moldy. You could also store mushrooms in paper bags or cotton mushroom bags as long as these are kept in an area with a low temperature to allow the mushrooms to last longer.

Now that you have a basic idea of the life cycle of mushrooms and how they are cultivated, we can begin getting our hands dirty. In the next chapter, I will show you the detailed, step-by-step process of growing mushrooms. I will be describing the processes of some beginner-friendly mushrooms, which include oyster mushrooms, shiitake, portobello and button mushrooms. Let's now delve into the mushroom-growing process together.

CHAPTER 5
Choosing Which Mushrooms to Grow

With this chapter, we begin looking at the step-by-step process of cultivating mushrooms, and the first step is choosing which mushrooms you want to grow. I will cover some of the mushrooms most commonly grown at home. This section will include a description of each of the mushrooms, which will aid you in identifying them, understanding how difficult they are to cultivate, and knowing where they are usually found in the wilderness. The types of mushrooms included in this section are widely regarded as beginner-friendly and are therefore the perfect fungi with which to start your mushroom growing journey, however before getting your hands dirty and growing mushrooms you can enjoy at home, let's first get into deciding which ones will suit your needs the best.

Factors to Consider When Choosing Mushrooms

When choosing which mushrooms you would like to grow at home, there are a few factors you need to take into consideration. The main factors we'll be looking at in this section include whether to grow your mushrooms indoors or outdoors, how long you will need to wait before seeing results, the amount of space you need to dedicate to your mushroom farm, and the climate and humidity levels of your area.

Indoor versus Outdoor Growing

As we looked at briefly in a previous chapter, some mushrooms grow better outdoors than they do indoors and vice versa; there are advantages and disadvantages to both environments. Certain mushroom types can be grown both indoors and outdoors, but you might find that they grow better in one than the other. In this section I will present you with the advantages and disadvantages of both areas and give you an idea of which mushrooms are more suitable to each environment.

Advantages to Growing Mushrooms Indoors

- · Growing mushrooms indoors takes up less room. All you need is a humid and dark spot. For example, you can grow your mushrooms in a cabinet or an unused corner of your basement.
- Indoor cultivation allows you to control the temperature of the environment to ensure the mushrooms grow properly.
- When growing mushrooms indoors, you can grow them all year long, resulting in a steady stream of mushrooms you can use for culinary and medicinal purposes.
- As growing mushrooms indoors allows you to control the growing environment more accurately, mushrooms grow faster indoors than they do outdoors.
- Growing your mushrooms indoors ensures you have a healthy, plentiful yield as you can constantly monitor the mushrooms and guarantee they are growing correctly.

Disadvantages to Growing Mushrooms Indoors

- Unless you have a large amount of space available, you will not be able to grow as many mushrooms as you would in an outdoor environment.
- Growing mushrooms indoors requires a lot of maintenance. You need to mist them with water and monitor your mushrooms daily. You will also need to check that the conditions remain optimal so as to not interfere with the growing process.
- You will have to keep close track of the growth and cycle of the mushrooms to ensure you harvest them on time. If you don't harvest the mushrooms before the spores are released, you will end up with thousands of spores in your house, which could aggravate allergies or other respiratory problems.
- When cultivating mushrooms indoors, you might find it difficult to maintain the proper humidity and temperature levels, which can have an adverse effect on the growth process if these are not at the right level.
- Mushrooms grown indoors can look quite different from their wild counterparts as it is difficult to reproduce the exact natural growing conditions.

Notwithstanding the above, most beginner-friendly mushrooms can be very successfully grown indoors; and include a number of mushroom variants such as reishi, lion's mane, cordyceps, button mushrooms and many more.

Advantages to Growing Mushrooms Outdoors

- Outdoor cultivation can be ideal in some cases as the existing environment already contains the ideal conditions without needing to control the climate.
- Growing mushrooms outdoors produces a much larger yield as you have more space in which to grow your mushrooms when cultivating them outdoors.
- You do not need to monitor outdoor growing mushrooms as closely as those grown indoors, as the ideal conditions are already naturally in place.
- The types of substrates usually used outdoors are nutrient-dense energy sources and are able to sustain the mushrooms for long periods of time.
- Growing mushrooms outdoors can be less expensive as you do not need specialized equipment in order to maintain the ideal climate.

Disadvantages to Growing Mushrooms Outdoors

- Outdoor cultivation is much slower compared to indoor cultivation as the natural climate is more unpredictable and conditions will fluctuate more often than the controlled environment created indoors.
- When growing mushrooms outdoors you are limited to growing only certain species, as not all homegrown mushrooms are able to be kept and cultivated outside.
- You will need to ensure the space where you are growing your mushrooms is protected against direct sunlight and drying winds, as these can be very damaging to mushrooms. This can prove to be a challenge if you don't have an area that is dark and humid outside.
- If the weather becomes dry, you will start to see your mushrooms disappearing until the conditions become favorable again, which could interfere with the growing process.
- Unlike the process of growing mushrooms indoors, outdoor cultivation cannot be maintained year-round. The natural climatic conditions for mushrooms grown outdoors fluctuate too often for them to fruit throughout the year.

Some of the best mushrooms to grow outdoors include Shiitake mushrooms, which can be grown on a log, White Button mushrooms that grow on compost, and the King Stropharia which enjoys growing in the sun.

Time Spent Growing Mushrooms

Mushroom species have different growing times, which means you might see some mushrooms mature before others. The physical time you will need to put into the cultivation process will never be more than a few hours each week, but the entire growth cycle takes some time and will differ from one variant to another. There is some dispute on exactly how long it takes for each mushroom type to reach the harvesting stage. The quickest growing mushrooms can be ready for harvest within four weeks while others take years to mature. This all depends on where you grow your mushrooms, which variants you grow, how you grow them, and so on. As a rule, the period of time in which mushrooms grow is generally measured from the inoculation to the forming of the fruit when they are ready to be harvested.

Space Needed to Grow Mushrooms

In general, you will not need a lot of space for a home mushroom farm. When growing indoors, a small area in a dark humid space is more than enough. If you are cultivating mushrooms outdoors, you will likely have more space at your disposal, which will likely allow for a larger yield. The amount of space you will need is dependent on the type of mushroom you are growing and your chosen substrate. Some substrates, like logs or stumps will take up more space than others. Growing mediums like straw, coffee grounds or bags will take up less space and therefore are great for growing mushrooms indoors. Provided you are not aiming to grow mass quantities of mushrooms or enough to sell to others, you will only need a space that measures around 2 square feet.

Climate and Humidity

The climate and humidity levels od your local area will influence which mushrooms you are able to grow outdoors. When growing mushrooms indoors, you have the ability to completely control the growing environment so the climate and humidity of the outside environment will not affect those mushrooms. However, you have very little control over the humidity levels and climate when growing mushrooms outside. Some mushrooms enjoy the sun and thrive in outside environments with fluctuating humidity levels while others are able to grow very well outside as long as they are kept in the shade.

Now that you know a bit more about the factors you need to consider when deciding which mushrooms to grow, we can take a closer look at some of the best mushrooms to grow at home, either indoors or outdoors.

Reishi Mushrooms

Reishi mushrooms are a wonderful mushroom to grow at home if you are looking to keep a medicinal species at hand. The reishi mushroom is known for its medicinal properties and is very beginner friendly. While these mushrooms are not as easy to grow as others, they are still one of the easiest species to begin with as they are strong colonizers and not likely to be contaminated. Reishi mushrooms, also known as Ganoderma lucidum, are saprotrophic fungi that feed on dying or dead hardwood trees and stumps. There are more or less 80 species of reishi mushrooms worldwide and they are known by different names in various regions. In this book, we will use the most popular name in the west, reishi.

Reishi mushrooms are also known as shelf fungi; the way in which they grow on trees tends to look like a colorful shelf protruding from the bottom of the tree trunk. When they first begin protruding from trunks and stumps, reishi mushrooms appear as slim, finger-like stalks known as antlers. These stalks can vary from rust brown to deep red, with tan, white and yellow tips. As the fruiting body matures, it flattens out to form a fan shape with a glossy, deep red body that transitions to orange, yellow and white towards the outside edge of the mushroom cap. The bottom of the mushroom cap houses yellow pores that release brown spores once it has completed its life cycle. Young mushrooms have a wet, shiny look which dulls and fades to a brown color as they age.

As reishi mushrooms are usually used for medicinal purposes, it is no wonder that taste is not what draws people to grow and use this mushroom. The taste is often described as bitter and unpleasant, and eating the reishi mushroom is akin to eating tree bark due to its tough, woody texture. Reishi is one of the easiest medicinal mushrooms to grow at home and offers a wide variety of health benefits. Reishis can aid in fighting viral infections and bacteria and boost your immune system. Traditionally, reishi mushrooms are made into a hot soup or tea consumed to fight infections, boost your immune system, and provide good antioxidants.

The colonization of reishi mushrooms takes place reasonably quickly as it takes the mycelium between one to two weeks to colonize the sawdust block completely. In contrast, colonisation will take much longer if you want to grow these mushrooms on logs. If you inoculate the logs using sawdust spawn, it can take up to 12 months for the reishi to fruit. Using plug spawn to inoculate the logs, it can take 18 months for the mushrooms to mature. reishi mushrooms grow slower in cooler conditions, so it will be better to cultivate them inside where you can control the temperature. When growing reishi mushrooms on logs it is best to begin the process in the spring; however you can still grow the mushrooms throughout the summer. As you begin to cultivate the reishi mushrooms, keep in mind that they grow best when the temperature is between 75°F and 85°F. Reishi grown outdoors will fruit early to mid-summer while those grown indoors can be grown throughout the year.

Oyster Mushrooms

There are a number of different Oyster mushrooms that can be grown at home and are beginner-friendly, although some still present more challenges than others. In this section I will introduce you to six different oyster mushroom variants you can grow at home for culinary or medicinal purposes. Oyster mushrooms are often considered to be one of the easiest species of mushroom to grow at home and are therefore one of the best to begin your mushroom-growing journey with.

Pearl Oyster Mushroom

The Pearl Oyster mushroom—also known as Pleurotus ostreatus, the gray oyster mushroom or the winter oyster mushroom—is one of the oyster mushroom variants most commonly available, making it one of the most popular strains of this species. This mushroom is grown for culinary purposes worldwide and can often be found in your local grocery store. Pearl oyster mushrooms get their name from two facets of their appearance: their color and shape. The color of the mushrooms is reminiscent of a pearl and can range from cream-colored to gray. The shape like other oyster mushrooms, is shell-like. Pearl oysters can be identified by their fan-shaped caps, lack of individual stems, and tendency to grow in clusters. Oyster mushrooms are saprotrophic, meaning they feed on dying or dead organic material. When growing naturally they are often found on logs and dying trees. Pearl oysters, like blue oysters, prefer cooler weather, which can easily be maintained when growing mushrooms indoors.

Though pearl oysters are genetically the same species as wild oyster mushrooms, they tend to look slightly different when cultivated at home compared to those grown in the wilderness. Oyster mushrooms of the same species you grow indoors will also look different than those you grow outdoors. Pearl oyster mushrooms are usually grown indoors and there isn't a lot of demand for foraged wild pearl oysters as they can easily be grown year-round. If you want to forage for wild pearl oysters, perhaps to gather spores to create spawn, it is best to look for them in the fall. In general, oyster mushrooms can grow in a range of climates, including subtropical climates and forests that experience a wide range of temperatures.

Pearl oyster mushrooms have a more prolonged incubation than other variants like phoenix oysters. Instead of taking between 10 to 14 days to incubate, pearl oyster mushrooms can take between 18 and 21 days. Unlike some other oyster mushroom varieties, pearl oyster mushrooms prefer cold weather and thrive between 53°F and 64°F. If you keep the growing climate within this temperature range, your pearl oysters will grow to be large and have darker, thicker caps. Should you grow your pearl oyster mushrooms in an area with a temperature above 64°F, the cap will grow to be a lighter gray color and the mushrooms will be smaller. Wild pearl oysters are easily noticeable after big, cooler weather changes, as you'll find them when foraging after a few rainy days or a frost. To avoid spreading too many of the pearl oysters' spores and perhaps developing allergies, harvesting them before they have fully opened prevents them from releasing their spores.

Pearl oyster mushrooms like other oyster mushrooms, have a handful of health benefits that add to the advantages of growing these at home. They contain a high amount of protein which means they can be a great meat substitute. Pearl oysters also have a variety of B vitamins, vitamin D, and every essential amino acid your body needs. In addition to this, pearl oysters are also high in fiber. It is believed that incorporating oyster mushrooms into your diet many facts help you lower high cholesterol and can aid in reducing the risk of cardiovascular disease. According to GroCycle's Adam Sayner, (2022) initial studies into the health benefits of oyster mushrooms indicate that they can aid in slowing the spread of certain types of cancer like colon or breast cancer.

Blue Oyster Mushroom

You won't often find blue oyster mushrooms, which makes them a wonderful and exciting species to grow at home. Like other oyster mushroom variants, blue oysters are easy to grow and are healthy and delicious. Oyster mushrooms are the easiest mushrooms for beginners to start with, and blue oysters are no exception. When looking for blue oyster spawn, you might find it by looking for its scientific name, Pleurotus ostreatus var. Columbinus.

When foraging for mushrooms, you can find blue oysters fairly easily. The color of their caps can range from a grayish color to light blue. The colour of the cap will be influenced by the growing conditions for the mushrooms and in particular the temperature. Blue oyster mushrooms have gills that run along the length of the underside of the cap and the mushroom's stem, and are a light gray color. As all oyster mushrooms look similar, the only obvious difference is their cap colors. The blue oyster mushroom is similar to other variants in terms of physical structure and shape. Younger blue oysters are blue when they begin pinning and then fade to gray as they mature. The cap of the blue oyster mushroom is generally thicker than the caps of other varieties.

Blue oyster mushrooms colonize the substrate fairly quickly, which means they fruit quickly. This leads to a demand for blue oysters for culinary use, so you could grow these mushrooms to sell at your local farmer's market and share these lovely blue fungi with others. When consuming blue oysters, you will find that the cap is the best part. With their thicker cap, blue oyster mushrooms have a meatier texture than other oyster mushroom species. The flavor of these mushrooms is often described as subtle; they have a savory, meaty flavor although others describe them as having a slight seafood flavor. In addition to these descriptions, blue oysters have been said to have a woody flavor similar to anise or mild licorice.

It is said that the blue oyster mushroom was first found in Europe, though it can now be found growing naturally in Asia, Europe, and North America. They are common in northern hemisphere forests and enjoy growing in humid biomes like mountains and forests. Blue oysters grow best in environments where humidity ranges from 50% to 70%. You will most likely find wild blue oyster mushrooms in the spring and fall. These mushrooms also thrive in cooler climates and prefer temperatures between 55°F and 65°F. Sometimes you will even see some blue oysters grow into the summer months if their environment allows it.

Like other oyster mushrooms, blue oysters grow on rotting, dying, or dead wood. They prefer growing on deciduous hardwood trees like oak or beech, but will grow on others if you don't have access to them. If you have a bit of experience or are a complete beginner, blue oysters are a relatively easy mushroom to grow. Blue oyster mushrooms grow quickly and produce a good yield. They are also ideal for growing outside if you live in a region that experiences cooler temperatures. Along with favoring cooler conditions, blue oysters also require plenty of fresh air and good airflow in the fruiting stage to allow for proper development. When growing blue oysters using a grow kit, the mushrooms can be ready to harvest in as little as two weeks.

If you decide to use premade spawn, you will have to wait slightly longer before being able to harvest your mushrooms. Blue oyster mushrooms can take up to three weeks to completely colonize the substrate. When the fungi have reached the fruiting stage you will need to maintain a temperature between 54°F and 64°F as higher temperatures might lead to misshapen mushrooms. Under the proper conditions, the mushrooms will form pins within seven days. After pins begin to form you will only have to wait another week before harvesting your fully-grown blue oyster mushrooms.

Phoenix Oyster Mushroom

The phoenix oyster mushroom has evolved to grow in a variety of warmer climates. It is therefore often known by names that reflect these, including the Indian oyster mushroom, the Italian oyster mushroom, and the summer oyster mushroom. Oyster mushrooms, varieties like the Phoenix Oyster included, are some of the easiest mushrooms to grow at home. Phoenix oysters are one of the more popular oyster mushroom variants to grow at home. The scientific name for the phoenix oyster mushroom is Pleurotus pulmonarius; "pulmonarius" is the Latin word for "lung," which relates to the shape of the mushroom. Due to its shape, this oyster mushroom is often called the lung oyster mushroom.

You can identify phoenix oysters by their shape or color, though the latter can be white or tan depending on the strain. The shape of phoenix oysters resembles the shape of other oyster mushrooms and they are shelf mushrooms with fleshy, fan-shaped caps. Before they mature, the edges of the caps curl underneath the cap but flatten out as the mushroom grows. In the wilderness you will find the phoenix oyster mushrooms in clusters of five or six mushrooms of varying sizes. The caps are usually between two and eight inches in diameter. Traditionally, the semicircular-shaped caps are beige or pale tan with lilac or gray undertones. Phoenix oysters have soft, white gills that run down the majority of the length of the stem. The white stems are off-center from the cap and are never longer than around 2.8 inches.

Unlike other oyster mushrooms, phoenix oysters will grow on both hardwoods and softwoods. Depending on the environment, these mushrooms can grow on softwood trees like spruce and fir and hardwood trees like poplar and elm. Phoenix oyster mushrooms get their nutrients from dead or decomposing organic matter. When foraging for these mushrooms you might find them in low-lying, humid areas near streams or ponds, or growing on decaying stumps or fallen logs. Phoenix oyster mushrooms can look very similar to other oyster mushrooms and the only way to identify them is by examining their microscopic spores. Luckily this doesn't often affect those growing mushrooms at home as it is much easier for beginners to buy spawn than make their own from mushroom spores.

In appearance and taste, phoenix oysters most closely resemble pearl oysters. The caps of phoenix oysters are often smaller and paler than pearl oysters and have longer, more noticeable stems. It is also rare to find phoenix and pearl oysters growing in the same area as phoenix oysters prefer warmer climates while pearl oysters favor cooler environments.

Out of all the variants of oyster mushrooms, phoenix oysters are the most beginner friendly. This mushroom can be grown in a range of substrates and is very sturdy and productive. If you grow phoenix oysters indoors you can create an optimal, warm environment and grow them year-round. Ideal fruiting conditions for phoenix oysters have a temperature between 64°F and 86°F, making them perfect for warm climates and growing during the summer. Depending on your farming method, phoenix oyster mushrooms can either be harvested within 14 days or take just over a month to reach the harvesting stage. Phoenix oysters can be grown both indoors and outdoors, and are a wonderful choice if you're looking for a mushroom that is both tasty and good for your overall health.

Pink Oyster Mushroom

The Pink Oyster mushroom is one of the most spectacular oyster mushroom variants, in appearance and growth. Pink oyster mushrooms are the quickest-growing variant of oyster mushrooms, and like other oyster mushrooms a great choice for beginner mushroom farmers. Wild pink oyster mushrooms can often grow on tropical hardwood trees in countries like Indonesia and Mexico, and areas with similar climates. Because pink oysters favor a warm, tropical-like climate, you will not find naturally growing pink oysters in colder climates such as most of Europe and North America. Luckily you can grow this warmth-loving mushroom year-round by cultivating it at home. In the wild, you will find pink oysters growing during the warmer months and even flourishing in the middle of the summer.

Under the right conditions pink oysters can begin producing fruit within only four weeks. When the mushrooms begin to grow from the ground you will be able to recognize them from their distinctive color and shape. In shape, pink oysters resemble other oyster mushrooms as they are shelf-like and have a fan-shaped cap. While pink oyster mushrooms grow in large clusters, the mushrooms themselves range from small to medium in size and the mushroom caps can be between 0.79 and 1.97 inches in diameter. You will be able to recognize pink oysters by their striking, vibrant pink color, and the top and bottom of the cap and the gills are pink. The color of pink oysters is at its most vibrant when the mushroom is young; as it matures it dulls to a soft, light pink color. During its life cycle, the pink oyster mushroom changes color multiple times. Not only does the vibrant pink dull as the mushroom matures, but its mycelium starts out white and then changes to pink as it grows and the mushroom becomes a cream or brown color when cooked.

Like all oyster mushrooms, pink oysters taste very bitter when consumed raw. To get the best taste from the mushrooms they need to be cooked properly. Compared to other oyster mushrooms, these have a mild taste characteristic for their species, but when compared to other mushroom species it has rich, deep flavor. You can use pink oysters as a vegetarian substitute for bacon; cook them until they are crunchy and brown, and the mushroom's texture could fool you into thinking you're having a bacon-filled meal. The conditions in which the mushroom is grown will affect its texture, making it either thick and meaty or thin and delicate. Pink oysters are usually more chewy or tough than other oyster mushrooms.

Achieving and maintaining proper ventilation and airflow can prove to be difficult when growing oyster mushrooms, but pink oysters are different. This mushroom type does not need a lot of fresh air so ideal conditions are a bit easier to maintain. If you want to speed up the colonization process, it is best to grow pink oysters on a straw substrate. For thicker and tougher mushrooms you can use a wood-based substrate. Pink oysters will produce fruit when the environment's temperatures range from 68°F to 86°F and the humidity levels are around 70%. Pinheads begin to form very early; it might look like the substrate has not been fully colonized yet when pinheads begin to form which can happen within a week. Pink oyster mushrooms usually begin producing fruit in three weeks. Once pinheads have begun to form, it can take between nine and fourteen days for the mushrooms to become fully-grown.

Golden Oyster Mushroom

The golden oyster mushroom, alongside the blue oyster and pink oyster, is known for its striking yellow color, and is often referred to as the yellow oyster mushroom. Golden oyster mushrooms are not only known for their color but also for their appearance which is reminiscent of the chanterelle mushroom. Golden oysters thrive in warmer temperatures, usually preferring an environment between 64°F and 86°F. When compared to other oyster mushrooms, golden oyster mushrooms are one of the smaller varieties, but what they lack in size they more than make up for by growing their eye-catching and colorful clusters. They have delicate thin caps which can be a range of yellow shades, from daffodil to golden. Due to it being an oyster mushroom, you can expect golden oysters to grow in shelf-like clusters with fan-shaped caps. You can spot these in the wild, but they are also one of the easiest mushroom species to grow at home. Golden oysters, when raw, have a spongy texture and can be bitter when consumed in this state.

This type of mushroom, part of the Pleurotaceae family, is an edible, gourmet mushroom with a taste some find difficult to describe as anything other than delicious. Though their flavors are more difficult to pin down, many have described golden oysters as either having a subtle, nutty flavor (like almonds or cashews) or a sweet, mild citrus and cinnamon-like taste. Out of all the oyster mushroom variants, golden oysters are the most aromatic. Once harvested they often resemble the smell of fresh watermelon, and cooked Golden oysters tend to smell like aged red wine. The texture of golden oyster mushrooms can range from smooth and velvety to meaty, crisp, and chewy. Like pink oysters they can be used as a bacon substitute, but lose their gorgeous yellow color once cooked, though they do keep their fan-like shape.

Golden oyster mushrooms are native to hardwood forests in eastern Russia, China, and Japan, and have more recently been growing in the wild in North America and Europe. The spread to different areas is attributed to production from small-scale farms, whereas farmers cultivate the mushrooms, the spores are able to release and spread into the wilderness. Like other oyster mushrooms, golden oysters are saprotrophic so they feed on dying and dead hardwood trees. They prefer growing on elm trees but are also often found growing on trees like beech, cherry, maple, and oak. As golden oyster mushrooms prefer growing in warmer temperatures, their ideal fruiting climate is an area with humidity levels of 85% or higher and temperatures between 65°F and 86°F. Though you can grow them throughout the year at home, you will also find them in the wild in the late summer and early fall. Golden oysters grow relatively quickly especially when using a growing kit and the mushrooms can be ready for harvest within two weeks. However, golden oysters can also be grown outside on logs, although this method can take six to twelve months for the fruit to appear.

When growing your own, you will find that golden oysters frequently fruit eagerly in dense clusters that can cover the tree stump they grow on. If you want to forage for wild golden oysters and begin your farm in this manner, there are certain features you can look for to ensure you're harvesting the right mushroom. The best way to identify these mushrooms is by looking at their caps; the caps are smooth with a velvety texture and can range from bright yellow to golden brown in color. A small indent in the center of the cap becomes more noticeable as they grow and gives the mushroom a funnel-like shape. The caps of mature golden oysters can fade to a pale yellow, off-white color. The gills are white or cream-colored, widely spaced and run down the stem. Golden oysters grow in dense, tight clusters when young, but grow further apart as they mature.

King Oyster Mushroom

The King Oyster mushroom is known by various English names, and many others worldwide, including French horn, king trumpet, royal trumpet, and scallop mushrooms. King Oysters are known by this name for two reasons: their taste is said to be superior to other oyster mushrooms and is the largest oyster mushroom species. This mushroom has a flat, thin cap and a thick stem, sometimes as wide as the cap. King oyster mushrooms and other oyster mushrooms are part of the same genus (Pleurotus), but are different species. While other oyster mushrooms have short stems, and oyster-shaped caps and form clusters, king oysters grow individually with white, thick stems and small tan-colored caps.

However, the conditions in which they are grown can significantly influence the king oyster's appearance. In the wild, king oysters grow to have large caps and small stems as they can access a lot of light and fresh air. When grown indoors king oysters tend to develop tall, wide stems and small caps due to the low light and little fresh air. Regardless, those that have grown and consumed king oyster mushrooms all agree that they are not only a unique mushroom but also a delicious one.

As with most oyster mushrooms, people find it difficult to describe the exact taste of the king oyster mushroom. Some find the taste of all oyster mushrooms similar to that of seafood, often describing this mushroom's texture and taste as similar to abalone, calamari or scallops. Others say it has a woody, slightly nutty taste or is savory and meaty. Finally, some say king oysters have a subtle licorice or anise flavor. King oyster mushrooms tend to have a meat-like texture and, when cooked in a certain way, can also have a mild meaty flavor. These mushrooms are also a good meat substitute often used by vegans because it retains their texture very well even when cooked. It can be used as a substitute for scallops or, when coated and fried, can have a chicken-like taste. King oysters are often grown year-round and indoors, which means you might be able to find them in your local grocery store, depending on where you live.

Though cultivated at home worldwide, King oysters can grow naturally in Central Asia, North Africa, Russia and Southern Europe. They thrive on the roots of decaying and dead deciduous trees. King Oyster mushrooms are both saprotrophic and slightly parasitic; they feed on dying or dead decaying matter and the roots of some herbaceous plants. You will spot king oysters growing from the soil in the fall and early winter. Their preferred fruiting conditions include humidity levels between 80% and 90% with temperatures ranging from 59°F to 65°F. The pins of king oysters form within eight days after colonization and will increase in size daily. If you are growing these mushrooms from scratch, you will need to factor in an additional two weeks of growth before they will be ready to harvest.

Shiitake Mushroom

While shiitake mushrooms are more challenging to grow than oyster mushrooms, cultivating these at home is more than worth the extra effort. Shiitake produces a good number of flushes, which means you will have an abundance of fresh mushrooms to harvest, and if you take care of the substrate and the growing conditions, you could be harvesting these for many years. Shiitake mushrooms are quite popular for culinary use, and you have likely seen this mushroom in your local grocery store. Though they have become well-liked in other cuisines, shiitake is a staple in many Asian cuisines, and it is clear why: they are delicious!

In Japanese, the word "shiitake" aptly describes what kind of mushroom this is: "shii" references the type of tree these mushrooms grow on, which is similar to oak, and "také" is the word for mushroom. Shiitake mushrooms have dark brown, large, umbrella-shaped caps that often appear black in color. They have tougher and thinner stems than portobello or cremini mushrooms, and the stems are usually cream-colored. The distinctive appearance of shiitake mushrooms means that you can recognize them quite easily. Shiitake mushrooms are not as common in places like North America as portobello or button mushrooms, but growing them at home will give you access to them year-round. You can find shiitake mushrooms growing in the wilderness throughout many regions in Southeast Asia. Shiitake mushrooms grow in the decaying wood of various deciduous trees including shii, chestnut, poplar, mulberry and maple. These mushrooms have been grown in China since the 13th century, and now they are grown across the globe, making up roughly a quarter of all mushrooms produced commercially every year.

Shiitake mushrooms have a much richer, more intense flavor than button and portobello mushrooms. Their taste is often described as meat-like and savory, with culinary experts referring to the flavor profile as umami. Like many other mushrooms, shiitake is an excellent meat substitute in vegetarian recipes. They can be used in place of ground beef in burger or lasagna recipes. For an even better flavor, you can also dry your mushrooms and use them in various culinary applications.

In addition to being delicious, shiitake mushrooms are nutritious and hold a number of health benefits. Traditional Chinese medicine, and some other health practices have been using shiitake mushrooms for hundreds of years. Shiitake mushrooms have many minerals and vitamins, including folate, vitamin B5, selenium, and zinc. They are a good source of fiber and are also low in sodium, fat-free, and cholesterol-free. Shiitake mushrooms are high in antioxidants and have important anti-inflammatory properties. As with other mushrooms, and all food in general, how you grow, store and prepare your mushrooms will greatly impact their nutritional content and how they benefit your health.

Because the mycelium of shiitake mushrooms is not as aggressive as the mycelium of other mushrooms, it takes longer to incubate, which does lengthen the process. The mushroom produces between three and five flushes on average if you grow them on grain or sawdust. If you grow them on logs, you can have fresh mushrooms roughly every five weeks for up to six years. For shiitake mushrooms to get the nutrients they need, it is best to use a wood-based substrate, which means you are limited to using blocks of sawdust or logs.

Lion's Mane Mushroom

Also known as Hericium Erinaceus, monkey's head mushroom or pom blanc, the lion's mane mushroom is a unique-looking fungus—it certainly doesn't suit the image we usually associate with a mushroom. Lion's mane mushrooms are large, pom-pom-like, and white. They have needle-like structures for gills that flow downwards as the mushroom grows, giving the fungi a bushy look very much like a lion's mane. Lion's mane has a spongy, soft texture and its internal structure is reminiscent of a cauliflower, with branches that extend from one central base. The lion's mane mushroom is native to Asia, North America, and

Europe, and you will find them growing on decaying hardwood logs and trees in the northern hemisphere. Though the legality of this mushroom has been questioned, lion's mane is perfectly legal. However, the mushroom is not widely known, and you are unlikely to find it in your local grocery store. If you want to try out this tasty mushroom, your best option is to grow it at home.

Lion's mane has a somewhat sweet, mild flavor that some consider similar to lobster or crab. Because the needles or teeth have a meat-like texture once cooked, this mushroom can be a great alternative to meat. The mushroom has finished growing when they no longer increase in size and the mushroom's spine grows thicker and longer. Lion's mane mushrooms need to be harvested before they turn brown or pink to experience all of its health benefits and for the best taste. For different textures, you can harvest your lion's mane at different stages of maturity.

Lion's mane mushrooms have a variety of health benefits and are considered one of many medicinal mushrooms. The mushrooms contain erinacine which is a substance that is believed to be able to enhance cognitive abilities through the initiation of regeneration and growth of nerves. Lion's mane can aid in reducing inflammation and lightening the symptoms of inflammatory bowel disease. In addition, the mushroom also has anti-inflammatory traits and is believed to have the potential to boost the immune system by amplifying immunity in the intestinal immune system.

Though lion's mane is seen as a beginner-friendly mushroom, there is a greater learning curve to the cultivation of this mushroom as the mycelium is incredibly fine. Because of this it can be difficult to discern when the substrate has been fully colonized and ready to begin producing fruit. If you are looking to cultivate mushrooms at home for the first time it might be better to begin with another mushroom species like oyster mushrooms and then once you are more comfortable with the process, you can grow lion's mane. Lion's mane mushrooms can be grown both indoors and outdoors, so you can decide which method works best for you and the space you have available.

As mentioned in a previous chapter, growing mushrooms outdoors takes much longer than growing them indoors and lion's mane is no exception. When grown outside on logs, it can take up to two years after inoculation for your first lion's mane mushrooms to be ready for harvest. However, once the mushroom begins producing fruit you can harvest mushrooms from the same log for roughly six years. If you choose to grow your mushrooms indoors instead, they will be ready for harvest far sooner. In around one month after inoculating the substrate, the lion's mane mushrooms should be ready to harvest. When incubating the inoculated substrate, the temperature of the climate needs to be between 68°F and 75°F to ensure the substrate is fully colonized. The colonization stage, during which the mycelium spreads through the substrate, takes between 14 and 21 days. Once the substrate has been fully colonized, pins will appear three days later. The pins will keep growing and fully-grown mushrooms will be ready for harvesting a week or two later depending on the temperature of the environment.

Cordyceps

The name of this mushroom originates from Latin and means "club head," which many deem to be an accurate description of the cordyceps. However, they are known by several other names worldwide, including Dong Chong Xia Cao in China, Yarza gunbu in Tibet and, in many English-speaking countries, caterpillar fungus. Over 700 species of cordyceps have been identified and most of these originated in Asia. Cordyceps mushrooms can be bright orange or brown and are one of the more strange-looking mushrooms. The mushrooms are long and spindly, and their caps resemble small clubs—hence the name "club head." Two particular variants, cordyceps sinensis and cordyceps militaris are particularly popular due to their medicinal properties.

While you will see that most, if not all of the mushrooms mentioned in this chapter prefer growing on dead trees or decaying organic matter, some cordyceps would instead grow on insects. Because of this, they are referred to as entomopathogenic or endoparasitoid fungi and it chooses mainly arthropods for their host. The most common host for cordyceps mushrooms is ghost mouth larvae. Cordyceps spores infect the caterpillar and take over its body, using its internal tissue as fuel. Once the caterpillar dies, the stroma of the cordyceps grows from the caterpillar's head. Cordyceps are most commonly found at higher elevations, so they are often found in a location like the Himalayan mountains, for example.

The most common way of growing these mushrooms at home involves using a solid substrate. Using this method, a material like rice or soy is sterilized and settled into growing containers before being inoculated with the mushroom's mycelium. Because cordyceps mushrooms need to be grown slowly at low temperatures you will need to add a filter to prevent contamination. Growing cordyceps this way will increase the number of beneficial compounds in mushrooms. It can take about a month for the cordyceps to sprout fruiting bodies and be ready to harvest.

Cordyceps mushrooms are mainly grown and used for their medicinal properties. These mushrooms have a long history of being used to treat ailments like chronic pain, liver and kidney disease, and tuberculosis. The beta-glucans in cordyceps aid in balancing and strengthening the immune system. It suppresses or stimulates immune responses depending on the body's needs. In addition to this, Cordyceps can help regulate gut immunity. It is also possible that some of the compounds found in cordyceps mushrooms can reduce inflammation as Cordyceps are full of antioxidants, which help combat inflammation.

White Button & Portobello Mushroom

Even if you haven't shown much interest in mushrooms before deciding to grow your own, I guarantee you have seen, interacted with, and perhaps even consumed white-button mushrooms. Agaricus bisporus, the white button mushroom, is one of the most popular mushrooms to cultivate and use in cooking. They are always in demand, widely available and inexpensive. Button mushrooms, portobello mushrooms, and cremini are all from this same species. Cremini mushrooms are a strain of white buttons but are brown instead, and portobellos are simply cremini mushrooms that have been left to mature longer.

These mushrooms have short, truncated stems, which attach to caps no more than two inches in diameter. The mushrooms range from small to medium in size and have rounded white caps which are firm and spongy. White button mushrooms have tiny, white, brown gills, hidden by a white veil. Both the cap and the stem of the mushroom are edible. Unlike some other mushroom species, button mushrooms are delicious when raw and when cooked. White button mushrooms have a mild flavor and crispy texture when raw, and when cooked they are more tender and chewier with an earthy flavor. In addition to being tasty, white button mushrooms also contain amino acids, antioxidants, folate, manganese, phosphorus, potassium, riboflavin, selenium, vitamin D, and zinc.

Unlike some of the other mushrooms mentioned in this chapter, it can be challenging to forage for white button mushrooms. The color of the mushroom is quite common; therefore, you risk harvesting poisonous mushrooms if you choose to forage for these instead of buying or growing your own. Unless you are an experienced forager and mushroom grower, it is better to stick to growing your own white-button mushrooms instead of looking for wild ones. Button mushrooms can be found in fields and grasslands worldwide and are known to appear from the ground after rain from spring to fall.

Though it is a great option for growing at home, cultivating white button mushrooms is much more complicated than growing say oyster or Reishi mushrooms because white mushroom cultivation involves working with compost. White button mushrooms are secondary decomposers so they cannot break wood down into compost and require other fungi to do so to be able to feed. Because of this, the process of cultivation can become quite complicated. White button mushrooms thrive in dark, damp, and warm conditions. As the mycelium grows, you will need to keep the temperature in the area at roughly 70°F. It is important to keep the substrate moist but not wet, as you would with other mushrooms. Once the mycelium has fully colonized the substrate, you can lower the temperature to 50°F. The button mushrooms should begin to sprout a month after colonization, and once the caps have popped open your mushrooms are ready for harvest.

We close this chapter with some basic information on white button mushrooms. You now have a veritable catalog of mushrooms you can grow at home. Before moving to the next step, it is a good idea to pause here for a moment and decide which mushrooms you would like to grow. Consider which ones best suit your needs, confidence level and available space. In the next chapter, we'll look at the importance of creating and keeping a sterile environment to avoid contamination and look at ways in which to combat contamination.

CHAPTER 6
Create a Sterile Environment

In this chapter, we move on to the next step in the mushroom cultivation process: creating and maintaining a sterile environment. It is incredibly important to keep the area in which you work with your mushrooms extremely clean. If the area where your mushrooms grow becomes contaminated; other fungi, viruses, and various bacteria can begin to invade your substrate and hinder the growth of your mushrooms. So, to keep your mushrooms safe, I will guide you through creating a sterile environment, and maintaining a sterile environment, and explain in more detail why this is so important. Additionally, this chapter will also teach you how to know when contamination has occurred, how to identify the type of contamination, and how to combat this.

Keeping a Sterile Environment

Growing mushrooms at home from scratch calls for a sterile environment, which needs to be maintained throughout the growing process for mushrooms to grow successfully. All the time and effort spent transferring cultures, inoculating substrate, maintaining the perfect climate, and so on can all be spoiled if a single mold spore enters the environment. Luckily, there are a few ways to minimize the risk of contaminants that can hinder growth or result in the death of your mushrooms.

Knowing where contamination comes from and how it can be mitigated may on the surface seem unnecessary. After all, mushrooms have been growing naturally in the wild for thousands of years. Circumstances, however are a bit different when growing your own mushrooms, as you want to be able to harvest a good yield of fresh mushrooms regularly and predictably. For example, fruiting blocks will give your mushrooms the nutrition they need to produce healthy, fresh fruit every time. Fruiting blocks aid us in forcing the mushrooms to grow as we want without having them compete for resources. Should that block become contaminated with another fungi spore, the two fungi will begin competing for nutrients and it is likely that the mushrooms will lose.

The exact cleanliness of the environment that is required will depend on a number of factors including the type of mushroom you are growing, the substrate you use, and where you are growing them; but it is always better to be overly cautious. That being said, it is impossible to create an environment that is 100% sterile all the time. You will constantly have to work towards creating a sterile environment, and will likely face challenges with contamination at least once, but if you know what to look for and you know how to combat it you greatly lower the risk of contaminants in your growing area in general.

Sterile techniques are some of the most important skills you will need to learn and develop to minimize the substrate's contamination risk. This involves keeping your tools, hands and work surfaces as clean as possible. All of this will aid in killing microbes that could potentially diminish your yields and compromise your crops. These techniques will minimize the number of microbes in the air while you transfer your colonized substrates for example. Lingering fungi or bacteria can latch onto substrates, Petri dishes, equipment, and so on, and feed on the nutrient crucial to mycelial and mushroom growth.

There are three different sources of contamination and each needs to be combatted in a particular way.

Airborne Contaminants

Your mushrooms can likely be contaminated by the air that cycles through the room you grow them in. Although fungi spores and contaminants are not visible without a microscope, they are everywhere, and likely to jump at the opportunity to move to the substrate and gather nutrients. The two most widely used methods to reduce the number of contaminants in the air involve using a laminar flow hood or a still air box (SAB).

Laminar Flow Hood

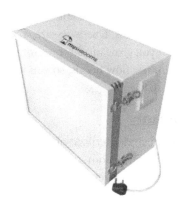

Laminar Flow Hood/Credit: www.myshrooms.co.za

This, along with a still air box, is one of the best methods of removing airborne contaminants. Be aware that flow hoods can be costly and time-consuming, whether you purchase one or build it yourself, and are only used by commercial growers. A laminar flow hood allows a stream of clean air to circulate through the room as you work with your mushrooms and can if used properly, eliminate contaminants. The device draws in air through a blower and passes it through a particle filter, trapping all unwanted spores. The resulting clean air passes over your workspace and pushes away microbes that could infiltrate your materials. Laminar flow uses a uniform current to push microbes away.

Still Air Box

Still Air Box/Credit: www.mycologist.art

In the coming section, I will discuss the still air box (SAB) in more detail, but here I am going to offer you a brief overview of this device. You can think of a still air box as a small, protected lab or a structure not dissimilar in shape to an incubator. In essence, a SAB is a large, see-through tote with holes cut into the sides. The inside of the tote is cleaned using alcohol and you slide your arms through the holes to work on your mushrooms. Due to its size, a SAB is far better for small-scale work and thus ideal if you grow mushrooms for personal use. Still air boxes are less expensive than laminar flow hoods, so you might want to consider this when deciding which one to use.

Substrate Contaminants

Improper or incomplete substrate sterilization before inoculation is a common cause of contamination in mushroom cultivation. Most substrates naturally contain organisms and dormant spores that can compete for the nutrients stored in the substrate. The amount of these natural competitors needs to be reduced significantly or eliminated completely to avoid losing nutrients. If they are not reduced, the organisms begin competing with the mushrooms for food, and the mushrooms are likely to come off second best. There are two ways the substrate can be treated to minimize the number of dormant spores and organisms. Below we will briefly touch on what some of these methods entail, but we will have a more in-depth discussion in a coming chapter.

Pasteurization

When using straw as a bulk substrate, it will need to be appropriately pasteurized to minimize the risk of contamination. Straw needs to be pasteurized for at least 90 minutes at a temperature between 149°F and 179.6°F. You can do this by using a large drum and a propane burner for manufacturing a hot water bath.

Sterilization

If you are using a sawdust fruiting block and mushroom grain spawn that has been supplemented, these need to be sterilized completely before inoculation can take place. This involves exposing the grain or substrate to high temperatures and pressures for an extended period of time. If you have a stovetop pressure canner large enough to hold the substrate and that can reach 15 PSI, you can sterilize the substrate at home. Grain spawn should be completely sterilized within 90 minutes, while supplemented sawdust fruiting blocks take roughly 2.5 hours.

Equipment Contaminants

It is incredibly easy to spread and pass on contaminants via your lab equipment, especially if you cultivate mushrooms using agar. More often than not, contamination is spread by improperly sterilizing your tools between culture transfers. You can mitigate this risk by using alcohol and flaming your scalpel between each transfer.

Using Alcohol

As a cultivator, you absolutely can only begin growing mushrooms by having and frequently using rubbing alcohol. You need to wipe down your tools and surfaces with rubbing alcohol before you begin working, and you should do the same between each transfer, especially when moving from one mushroom species to another. In addition to this, rubbing alcohol can be used to wipe down agar plates prior to opening, grain jars, and the outside of grow bags. For ease of use, it is recommended you purchase a lab-style bottle of rubbing alcohol as this allows you to use the right amount without having to pour it from a bottle with a large mouth, which is more difficult to control.

Flame Your Scalpel

As strange as this may sound, scalpels need to be flame sterilized between every single transfer. This entails keeping your scalpel in a flame for no more than 30 seconds or until it glows red. The scalpel will cool instantly once returned to the agar. Though you can achieve the same results with a lighter, it is much easier to flame sterilize with an alcohol lamp.

Culture Contamination

Despite creating and maintaining the perfect sterile environment, you will eventually be faced with culture contamination, at some point or another. This section deals with identifying contaminations, which types of contamination you can expect to encounter and what to do when contamination has occurred.

Identifying Contamination

Trichoderma/Green Mold

Some obvious physical indications and differences in appearance will alert you to the fact that your mushrooms have been contaminated. Below is a list of things you can look out for. If you experience any of these, your mushrooms will likely be contaminated.

- It develops a strange odor. This is generally the first sign of contamination. While the mycelium might retain its white color when contaminated, if it or your substrate develops an unexpected, strange new smell it has been contaminated.

- Parts of the mushroom culture become slimy. Common bacteria that contaminate mushroom cultures make the contaminated areas appear slimy. You will be able to see this as a brownish residue around grains or in places where the mycelium presses against the container.

- Borders begin to develop between two mycelia. This indicates sectoring which means two fungi are growing simultaneously and are fighting for nutrients and space.

- The mycelium, pinheads, or fruiting bodies discolor. Because mycelium is generally white and each mushroom has a distinct color, discoloration can often indicate contamination. A slightly different tinge should not be taken as a definitive indication; but if the color begins to spread, it is likely that your mushrooms have been contaminated. Look out for unexpected spots of blue, green, yellow or white. Take note that blue could also indicate bruised mycelium and yellow can mean the mycelium is old and creating new defenses.

- Your mushrooms become spongy and smooth. When this happens, it means the contaminant (likely mold) has filled the volume of the container. This is an indication that the contaminant is spreading through the substrate.

- If your mycelium appears dusty, it could mark the invasion of a contaminant. In order to spot these, you will need to use a magnifying glass to examine the mycelium closely

Examples of Contamination and How to Manage Contamination

As contamination tends to spread incredibly quickly, it would be better to move the contaminated cultures away from non-contaminated cultures. Some common contaminants target mushrooms or are often encountered during the cultivation process. Once you know what these contaminants are and how to tackle them, being faced with contamination is less daunting. In this section, we'll take a closer look at some of the most common contaminants, how to identify these and what to do once they have been identified.

Cobweb Mold

This is not one singular species of mold; rather, it is a group of closely related mold species that when contaminating substrates, leads to soft rot in mushrooms. When using grain spawn, you are likely to encounter cobweb mold at some point. It can be difficult to identify cobweb mold because its appearance is very similar to that of mycelium. Cobweb mold appears white, gray, and fuzzy, similar to mycelium. However, the mold is often greyer and wispier than mycelium. It has extremely fine strands that differ from mycelium's rope-like appearance and is said to smell like mildew. If you are confronted with wispy, grayish tufts growing upwards in your substrate when you open the growing container, it is probably cobweb mold.

Cobweb mold can also be identified by the extreme speed with which it grows. A tiny patch can take over the entire container in no more than 48 hours. The patches of this mold are light and thin when compared to the vibrant patches of white that make up the mycelium. Usually the cobweb mold appears to levitate above the substrate, grows very three-dimensional and can be distinguished from mycelium as it tends to grow above the substrate rather than throughout.

You can minimize the chances of coming across cobweb mold by ensuring your substrate is not overhydrated. Cobweb mold thrives in high humidity levels, and an overhydrated substrate is generally the result of high humidity. You can limit the initial contamination and spread by lowering the humidity levels and providing better air circulation. If you spot cobweb mold early, you can control the spread and potentially save your mushrooms by using a hydrogen peroxide spray. The spray will not harm the mycelium, but will kill mold and spores that attempt to eradicate your mushrooms.

Wet Spot

Wet spot, also known as sour rot and bacillus spp, is the most common type of bacterial mushroom contamination. This type of bacterial contaminant is commonly found in grain substrates. With a consistency similar to that of mucus, the wet spot is slimy, dull gray and excessively wet. In addition, grains begin to smell sour once the bacteria have infiltrated the substrate. A wet spot usually presents as a slimy, uncolonized patch and can be found at the bottom of the growing container.

To combat this bacterial contamination, cultivators often soak the grains for up to 24 hours before sterilizing or hydrating them. Bacterial endospores are often heat resistant and survive the pressure cooking process. This problem can be circumvented by soaking the grains, allowing bacterial endospores to awaken and germinate. When sterilization temperatures are reached during the pressure-cooking process, the now awake endospores are killed. If you skip the soaking process, the endospores remain dormant and live through the sterilization process, allowing them to come alive after the grains have been inoculated and allowing them to infect your mushrooms.

It is possible to separate grains contaminated by bacteria from non-contaminated grains, but this is only viable when the bacterial patch is still small and kept to one area. Using a flame sterilized or an alcohol-sanitized spoon, you can scoop the patch out of the grain. When working with Petri dishes, it can be a good thing to experiment with wet spot contamination, should it occur. If your mycelium culture consumes the bacteria, you have a strong culture that is able to fight off the bacteria. If the bacteria destroy your mycelium, you can separate the contaminated culture from the non-contaminated cultures and take extra care to soak the grain before sterilizing the substrate.

Green Mold

Also known as Trichoderma, green mold can cause damage to your yield because it grows incredibly quickly and steals the nutrients your mushrooms require for proper growth. Green mold overcrowds the substrate, leaving less growing space for your mushrooms and an inadequate amount of important nutrients. This contaminant targets and preys on mycelium. The aggressive white mycelium causes soft decay, and turns a vibrant green once it sporulates. Green mold is one of the easiest contaminants to identify but also one of the most difficult to eliminate.

Green mold needs to be identified before inoculation because it becomes increasingly more difficult to save your crop after this stage. In the growth stage right before inoculation, green mold can look similar to mycelium to the untrained eye. However, the green mold is fluffy and thick, and appears to rise from the substrate. Mycelium remains close to or intertwined in the substrate and is more rope-like.

It is virtually impossible to contain green mold once it has taken hold of the substrate. When it inoculates, you will need to remove the contaminated container as far away from your other mushrooms and workstation as possible. If you do not remove it from the area, you risk contaminating everything as it spreads easily and quickly. If you are determined to attempt to save the contaminated fungi, you can spread salt on the affected area. However, this is only successful in some cases and with certain mushroom species. All things considered, it might be wiser to cut your losses if this occurs, and dispose of the contaminated mushrooms.

Black Mold

Black mold is the contaminant you are least likely to encounter. Fruiting blocks or containers infected with black mold should be removed from your home or workplace immediately as it can have an adverse effect on those with breathing difficulties, allergies, and asthma. Unlike some of the other contaminants already mentioned, black mold grows slowly. Much like cobweb mold, this mold flourishes in a wet environment; overwatering your substrate can create the ideal conditions for black mold to grow.

The mold lives up to its name as it is a dark black and, when touched, will feel moist. Black mold can be found in any organic substrate, so you can expect to be confronted with it when working with agar and grain cultures. There are different species of black mold and the colors range from black to yellow, though the one we are most concerned with is dark black; this is one of the species which releases toxins and harms those with the ailments mentioned above.

If your substrate or fruiting block becomes contaminated with black mold, even if only a small spot appears, it is best to dispose of the entire container or block immediately. When growing in other areas in your home there are ways in which it can be removed, but the same is not true for growing containers. Once a block or container has become contaminated, mushrooms will not grow at all and you only risk harming yourself and spreading the mold to other mushrooms.

Orange Bread Mold

In the world of mushroom cultivation, orange bread mold is commonly referred to as "farm killer." It grows and spreads at an impressive speed, quickly overwhelming your mushroom farm and making it difficult to eliminate. Whether you are growing for personal or commercial use, once you find this contaminant in your farm it needs to be removed immediately. Orange bread mold is often present in subtropical and tropical areas, but will also grow during warmer months and in humid or hot regions.

Orange bread mold, unlike black mold, is harmless to animals and people but grows quickly enough to overtake mycelium completely. This mold is bright orange and is fine and wispy when it first appears but grows into a neon orange, powdery patch. If you don't remove the mold, it forms round, lumpy, orange structures. You will need to remove it when it is still wispy as it has not yet released spores in this form.

The source of the orange bread mold needs to be contained in a sealed plastic bag and discarded as soon as possible. Once it has appeared and if left untreated, it takes only eight hours for it to take over the substrate and begin spreading through the air. When removing the mold, be as gentle as possible and avoid disturbing it; when disturbed, it releases a light cloud of orange spores. As it grows in materials like compost, coffee grounds and damp, untreated wood, you need to remove these from the workspace as they can be the source of the orange bread mold.

Now that you are more familiar with a few common contaminants, let's take a closer look at still air boxes. SABs will aid you in creating a sterile environment thereby mitigating the risk of contamination. Still air boxes are relatively inexpensive, and you can even make your own at home.

Everything About the Still Air Box

Still air boxes (SAB) are closed boxes with a window containing two holes for your arms that allow you to work with the cultures placed inside without subjecting them to other bacterial or fungal spores that could cause contamination. SABs are sterile enough to allow mushrooms to grow and flourish as needed. The main purpose of a SAB is to create an environment that is semi-sterile. I say semi-sterile because without careful care and maintenance the culture you work with can still become contaminated. This structure is used to maintain a pure environment in which mushrooms can be grown without fear of having to compete with other fungi. If you are a beginner when it comes to mushroom cultivation, I strongly advise you to use a SAB. When growing your own mushrooms, a still air box is crucial to growing the best possible mushrooms.

Still Air Box or Flow Hood?

We've discussed flow hoods in a previous section of this chapter, but between laminar flow hoods and SABs, which one is best for mushroom cultivation? Ultimately, how you create a sterile environment is up to you. Knowing more about each of these methods will allow you to make an informed decision.

Flow Hood

If you are concerned about contamination and wish to make this a priority in your cultivation process, you might prefer flow hoods over SABs. Some studies indicate that flow hoods are better at reducing contamination than a still air boxes. The air in a still air box is calm and still. In contrast, flow hoods provide an uninterrupted, sterile airflow that removes spores or bacteria from the air and preserves the integrity of the mushroom culture. I will not be going into too much detail regarding the flow hood as I strongly advise against beginners purchasing a laminar flow hood. They are far more expensive than still air boxes which you can make at home; still air boxes can cost as much as $20 while flow hoods cost $500 or more.

Still Air Box

While a SAB is not 100% sterile, it is very efficient in preventing contaminants from entering the box. While setting up the box, especially when building one yourself, it is likely that a few microbes will make their way inside the box. Keep in mind that your mushroom cultures can be contaminated to begin with, so the lack of a sterile environment is one of many causes of contamination. Despite this, SABs nevertheless keep the air inside the box calm and still. The environment inside the box is semi-sterile and using a still box is very convenient.

Making and Sterilizing a Still Air Box

As mentioned, you can make your own still air box at home, and whether you purchase or make one, you will need to sanitize and sterilize the SAB before using it for the first time. To maintain a sterile environment, it is best to sterilize the SAB in between working with different cultures whether from the same species or not.

Making Your Own SAB

You will need the following:

- A clear plastic container with a lid
- A marker
- Sandpaper
- A metal can wide enough in diameter to create the armholes
- A heat source like a butane torch

When you have gathered all of your supplies, you can begin making your SAB. The steps are as follows:

1. Working at a table, turn the container upside down and place it on the table.

2. On the length of the container, use your hands or forearms and the marker to indicate where the armholes will be. Remember that both openings must be on the same side of the SAB.

3. To make the above step easier, place your arms as you would when writing. This will indicate how far apart the holes need to be. Mark this position.

4. Heat the bottom of the can until it is incredibly hot. It should be able to burn through the plastic container.

5. Keeping the container upside down, use the can to create the armholes. Apply pressure to the container and the can should melt through the plastic. Once one hole has been made, you can repeat the process to make the second hole.

6. Once both holes have cooled down, lightly sand the inside of the holes so there are no sharp edges that can hurt you.

Now that you have made your one still air box, you can sterilize the container. Once this is done, you are one step closer to beginning your cultivation process. You will need the following:

- Bleach
- A white towel
- 70% Isopropyl alcohol
- Paper towels
- Latex gloves
- Plastic sheeting

Sterilize the SAB as follows:

1. Mix one ounce of bleach with two quarts of water. Dip a paper towel into the solution and allow it to soak it up.

2. Spray the inside of the container with the alcohol, allow it to dry and, as an extra measure, wipe it down with a paper towel to ensure it is dry.

3. Repeat the above step with the lid of the container.

4. Put the gloves on and remove the paper towel from the bleach solution. Squeeze out as much moisture as possible.

5. Spread the towel over the inside of the closing lid. Check that there are no bumps or wrinkles.

6. Turn the air box upside down and place it on top of the lid, keeping the towel on the inside.

7. Cut the plastic sheets so they fit the armholes; the sheets should be the same size as the longer side of the container. Once cut, spray them with alcohol and wait for them to dry.

8. Drape the sheets over the armholes and tape them to the box to ensure it stays attached to the SAB and covers the holes entirely.

9. You now have a SAB in which to cultivate your mushrooms.

As we close this chapter, you now know how important a sterile environment is to mushroom cultivation. You also know how to identify various contaminants and how to save your mushrooms from being destroyed by these. In the next chapter, we move on to the third step in growing your own mushrooms, which will focus on preparing the mushroom spawn.

CHAPTER 7
Preparing the Mushroom Spawn

So, you have decided which mushrooms to grow and know how to keep the growing environment sterile and conducive to growth. However, before you begin growing mushrooms and using your sterile environment, you will need to pick out and prepare mushroom spawn. In this chapter, I will guide you through identifying the best spawn for your chosen mushrooms and how to obtain the correct one. By the end of this chapter, you will be able to identify the different most commonly used spawn and know which will allow your mushrooms to thrive.

Mushroom Growing Kits

Before we get into the various mushroom spawn available to you, let's take a quick look at mushroom growing kits, what they are, and how they work. For many beginner cultivators, it is much easier to grow mushrooms with a grow kit. Mushroom growing kits serve as a learning model for beginners. With a grow kit, you do not have to be concerned about sterile production methods, developing a growing room, or creating and maintaining cultures. Suppose you are interested in growing your own mushrooms but not confident enough to invest a lot of time and effort into a longer cultivation process. In that case, growing kits are a good investment and a way to experiment with mushroom cultivation before dedicating many resources. You will see that, as a beginner, it can be much easier to grow all your mushrooms using a kit. However, bear in mind that it can be more expensive in the long term if you decide to grow mushrooms this way.

How Growing Kits Work

Traditionally, mushroom grow-kits include a growing medium that has already been inoculated with mushroom spawn. Grow kits are complete packages that only require moisture and a dark area to begin growing. No matter the type of mushroom growing kit used, all work in the same general manner; they attempt to imitate the natural conditions in which mushrooms grow. The substrates need to be moist; the temperature is lower at night and, along with certain other mushroom-specific conditions, the mushrooms begin to grow.

When you purchase and use mushroom grow kits, all of the time-consuming work involved in preparing the substrate has already been done for you. There is no need to prepare, pasteurize, sterilize, or inoculate substrate as this has all been done. In the kit, you receive a substrate that has already been inoculated and colonized. Mushroom growing kits provide you with easy-to-follow instructions that aid you in creating the ideal conditions in which the mycelium can begin to produce fruit. The mycelium provided in the kit need only be kept in the correct environment for triggering pinning. If the ideal conditions are maintained, you will soon have mushrooms.

Airflow, humidity, light, and temperature are all important factors to consider when creating the ideal growing conditions. The exact conditions will differ from mushroom species to mushroom species, but these factors remain important regardless of the type of mushroom. Usually the substrate block, log, or whatever other substrate the mushrooms prefer, comes in a bag. Often you will need to alter the bag or completely remove the substrate block from the bag to create the perfect growing environment.

To maintain the proper airflow, you will need to create a window in the substrate bag or, depending on the species' requirements, remove the substrate block from the bag entirely. Regarding lighting and temperature, a spot near a window that is relatively warm and experiences 12 hours of indirect sunlight each day should allow for ideal fruiting conditions to occur. If you mist the mycelium, pinheads, and fruiting bodies as they grow, the required humidity levels will be maintained throughout the growing cycle. Some species are more particular about the conditions they grow in, and you will need a fruiting chamber to aid in producing and maintaining the conditions required for growth. If this is the case, the kit should indicate the need for a fruiting chamber.

Which Mushrooms can be Grown Using Growing Kits?

Certain mushroom types are grow-kit friendly and are not too picky about the conditions in which they grow, but some species prove to be very difficult to grow using a kit. In this section, we'll look at some easy-to-grow mushrooms when using a growing kit, and some of the mushrooms that are more difficult to grow with grow kits.

When cultivating mushrooms at home, cultivators generally gravitate towards mushrooms that you would not find in your local grocery store. This is true for growing kits as well. Most grow kits contain spores and substrates for mushrooms not readily available other than in the wild. Mushroom growing kits can be utilized indoors and outdoors, like growing mushrooms from scratch. The following is a list of mushrooms that are easy to grow and thrive when using a growing kit:

- Button mushrooms
- Chestnut mushrooms
- Cremini mushrooms
- Enoki mushrooms
- Lion's mane
- Maitake mushrooms
- Most oyster mushroom variants
- Pioppino mushrooms
- Reishi
- Shiitake mushrooms

The mushrooms mentioned above make for very good growing kits and most, if not all, are beginner friendly. Unfortunately, not all mushrooms work with growing kits. In general, these mushrooms are a bit more difficult to grow at home whether with a kit or from scratch. These are as follows:

- Boletes
- Chanterelle mushrooms
- Morel mushrooms
- Truffles

These mushrooms are difficult to grow for a variety of reasons. It might not be easy to maintain the ideal conditions as they may take years to fruit, or they are simply not entirely suited for small-scale home growth.

If you are interested in using mushroom growing kits, whether as a beginner or an expert, there are various ways to obtain such a kit. Websites like Amazon, GroCycle, and North Spore sell growing kits online, and you might occasionally find growing kits in large chain grocery stores.

Using Premade Spawn to Grow Mushrooms

In essence, mushroom spawn is any material that has been inoculated with mycelium and is then used to grow mushrooms. Mycelium is the base needed to grow mushrooms; without one, the other would not exist. Using spawn, mycelium is transferred onto the substrate, which will allow the mycelium to begin forming fruiting bodies. Mushrooms can be grown from spawn without using the substrate, though this method is not ideal as using spawn alone will result in a smaller yield. If you do not want to use a growing kit and are yet confident enough or able to grow your own spawn, it is best to obtain premade spawn from a supplier. Often, established cultivators sell spawn to beginner and experienced mushroom growers.

Buying Premade Spawn vs Growing Your Own

There are advantages to both growing your own spawn and buying premade spawn. Choosing which method to use depends on various factors: what mushrooms you want to grow, the size of your mushroom farm, your experience and so on. If you are an absolute beginner, it will be easier to buy premade spawn than to learn how to grow your own. Buying premade spawn is often far less intimidating than spending the time and effort to learn how to grow spawn. Below are some benefits of both methods.

Buying Premade Spawn

- There are a variety of mushroom spawn producers that sell their products online and in offline stores. The ease with which it can be bought is an advantage of using premade spawn.

- Premade spawn can be used as soon as it has been purchased. You save some time by buying instead of making spawn, meaning you can expect to see results sooner.

- Using premade spawn is ideal when growing mushrooms for personal use. You can purchase enough spawn to produce the perfect number of mushrooms to fulfill your individual needs and you do not need to develop the skills required to grow your own spawn.

Growing Spawn

- Growing your own spawn is less expensive than buying premade spawn. You will have to invest some money when beginning the process, but growing your spawn will be the more financially responsible method in the long term.

- You have more control over the mushroom species you can grow. When producing your own spawn, you are not limited to certain types of mushrooms; you can choose which you would like to grow instead of only being able to choose from those the supplier has available.
- Growing your own spawn creates the opportunity for a bigger yield. Because you can create more spawn, you can grow more mushrooms. This is especially beneficial when you want to sell mushrooms to your neighbors or at your local farmers' market. For the same amount of time and money invested, you can grow more mushrooms.

Based on these advantages, you can decide which method best suits your space, goals, and needs. However, if you are a complete beginner, I would advise you first to use premade spawn and become familiar with how it works before attempting to grow your own.

Different Types of Premade Spawn

The spawn can be seen as the carrier of a specific strain of mycelium, which will eventually grow into a particular mushroom species. The spawn keeps the mycelium in stasis until it is ready to be transferred to a substrate. Once transferred, the mycelium can colonize the substrate and begin to form pinheads which will grow into fully developed mushrooms. Different mushroom species will prefer different types of spawn. In this section, we'll take a closer look at various commonly used types of premade mushroom spawn.

Grain Spawn

Grain is one of the materials most frequently used to produce spawn. The spawn comprises sterilized grains inoculated with sterile mycelium culture or mushroom spores. Grain spawn can be used in various ways, including making more grain spawns, sawdust spawns, or inoculating specific pasteurized substrates. Mainly, grain spawn is used to inoculate looser substrates like straw and is known to provide extra nutrients to substrates that have yet to be supplemented. You can use a variety of grains to create the spawn such as millet, rye, wheat, corn, and cereal grains. A benefit of using grain is that it is more nutritious than sawdust which makes it ideal for inoculating indoor-type substrates. On the other hand, grain should not be used to inoculate outdoor beds as it can attract critters like rodents or birds.

Sawdust Spawn

This spawn is made up of sterilized sawdust. The pieces of sawdust are no more than a few inches in diameter and reasonably coarse. In addition to this, sawdust is generally made out of a type of hardwood. You can use sawdust spawn to inoculate several substrates including outdoor beds, cardboard, and logs, and can be used to inoculate wooden dowels to produce plug spawn. On the one hand, sawdust spawn has copious amounts of tiny particles, meaning there are numerous inoculation points through which the mycelium can grow into the substrate. This speeds up the colonization process, shortening the window of time in which contaminants can invade the substrate. On the other hand, sawdust spawn on its own does not possess an adequate number of nutrients for proper mushroom growth. For this reason, you should avoid growing mushrooms from straight sawdust as you will be sorely disappointed by the results.

Plugs and Dowels

Plug or dowel spawn comprises wooden dowels inoculated with your chosen mycelium. The dowels are traditionally 5/16 x 1-inch pieces of wood that the mushroom mycelium has colonized. Plug spawn dowels need to be hammered into logs. Hardwood dowels can easily be inserted if you drill holes first. After the log has been inoculated, you will need to seal the inoculation site with wax to keep the plug from drying out. Plug spawn is quite tough and long-lasting and is a very reliable medium if you plan on growing mushrooms that take longer to complete their life cycle. However, plug spawn is often more costly than sawdust spawn even though both have the same inoculation rates.

Thimble Spawn

This type of spawn is essentially sawdust spawn that has been formed into thimble-shaped pellets and then covered with a thin foam cap. The cap seals and protects the spawn, keeping it from drying out and removing the need for a wax sealant. Like plug spawn, thimble spawn is mainly used for inoculating logs, so you will need to drill small holes into the logs and then simply insert the thimble spawn using your fingers. Thimble spawn only need as much supervision as other types while allowing the mycelium to spread quickly and efficiently. The spawn is bigger than plug spawn so you can expect the colonization time to be the same as sawdust spawn, making it a bit quicker than plug spawn. However, thimble spawn is known to dry out in climates that do not experience a lot of rain.

Other Types of Mushroom Spawn

There are a number of other types of mushrooms spawn, most of which are only used when growing a certain species of mushrooms. These include:

- Peg spawn
- Straw spawn
- Wood chip spawn

Which Spawn to Use

As mushroom spawn is used to transfer the mushroom's mycelium to a suitable substrate, you must choose the proper spawn material. For example, some mushrooms can only grow on a hardwood substrate like oak logs and some spawn is more suited than others to aiding growth on this kind of substrate. Therefore, it is crucial that you select the spawn based on the mushroom you are planning to grow and the substrate you will use. When choosing spawn, it is also important to note that it needs to be used within a certain period of time, and for that reason premade spawn bags have a "use-by" date. The date will indicate how long you have to transfer the spawn to an appropriate substrate.

During our discussion regarding spawn in this chapter, you will notice that I have only briefly referred to making your own spawn. In an upcoming chapter we'll take a more in-depth, step-by-step look at how to make your own spawn. This chapter focuses on first understanding the types of premade spawn available to you and how to choose the appropriate spawn. In the next chapter, we will move on to step four of the cultivation process, which involves learning more about the substrate and preparing the substrate for inoculation and incubation.

CHAPTER 8
Preparing the Substrate

O nce you have determined what type of mushrooms you would like to grow and which spawn to use, you can move on to the next step in the cultivating process, which is choosing and preparing a substrate. In this chapter you will have the opportunity to become more familiar with various types of substrate and the processes involved in getting the medium ready for the next step. So, without further ado, let's get ready to choose and prepare mushroom substrate.

What is Substrate?

In the wilderness, mushrooms grow from the soil, on the sides of trees, or on decaying logs. As much as we want to mimic these natural conditions when growing mushrooms at home, it is not always possible. So, to produce a yield that best suits our personal needs, we turn to substrates. In essence, the substrate is to mushrooms what soil is to plants, namely the material through which their roots, or mycelium in the case of mushrooms, spread and take up nutrients. As with soil, the higher the quality of the substrate used, the healthier your mushrooms will be, and you can expect a plentiful yield. If the mycelium does not have access to the proper environment, you will not see any fruiting bodies appear no matter how much you take care of the substrate.

As briefly mentioned in the previous chapter, you absolutely can grow mushrooms straight from the spawn without transferring them over to the substrate, but you will always have a much better chance of success if you transfer the spawn to the substrate. Many cultivators prefer transferring spawn to the substrate for various reasons: the substrate aids in providing the ideal environment for mushroom growth, and the mycelium can properly expand and retrieve the needed nutrients and water and can therefore produce a healthy yield.

Different mushroom species prefer different substrates and although there is some flexibility, (i.e., some species thrive in multiple substrates), it is important to take the time and choose a substrate that best accommodates your chosen mushrooms. While mushroom species usually have an ideal substrate that allows for optimal growth, as you become more familiar with the growing process you can experiment with different substrates. Some of the most commonly used substrates include hardwood sawdust, coffee grounds, logs, and coco coir. In the following section, we'll look at the most used substrates you can choose. Keep in mind that some mushrooms grow comfortably on a number of these substrates while others prefer a specific medium.

Choosing a Substrate

It is incredibly important to choose a substrate that will be able to adequately fulfill your mushroom's needs and provide it with the opportunity to grow and produce a good amount of fruiting bodies. Some substrates are used more often than others and provide better results making them incredibly popular in the cultivator community. In this section, I will introduce you to various substrates you can choose from, providing descriptions for each and giving examples of mushrooms that grow best in each substrate.

Cardboard

Cardboard as a substrate is one of the most commonly used mediums by those who grow mushrooms at home. With a few minor modifications you can recycle some of the cardboard you have in your home and use it to grow mushrooms. Due to the wood-based nature of cardboard, it can be reasonably nutritious and often has similar levels of nutrition to some hardwood substrates. Cardboard is incredibly inexpensive compared to other substrates, and you can often find cardboard for free. Mushrooms that can be grown on cardboard substrates include golden and pink oyster mushrooms. All you need to do to prepare the substrate is to soak it in boiling water, remove it, and let it cool. Once cooled, squeeze out any remaining water. Once you have done this, the substrate is ready to be colonized with mushroom spawn.

Coco Coir and Vermiculite

Coco Coir//Credit: www.sporeshift.co.nz

Vermiculite//Credit: www.sporeshift.co.nz

Coco coir substrate is made from ground-up coconut shells and husks while vermiculite is a mineral that aids in retaining moisture and aerates the substrate mixture. Mix one part vermiculite with one part coco coir to prepare the substrate. When obtaining coco coir, you will find it comes as a brick. You will have to add boiling water to soften and expand it enough to allow the mycelium to colonize the substrate. You should add equal amounts of boiling water and dry ingredients. Allow the mixture to cool completely before adding the spawn. Coco coir alone will not make for an effective substrate, so it should be mixed with vermiculite. Please note that coco coir expands when water has been added to it, so you will end up with more substrate than you might think. Several mushroom species can be grown using this substrate mixture including oyster mushrooms and psilocybe cubensis.

Coffee Grounds

Like cardboard, coffee grounds are an excellent substrate material for those growing mushrooms at home who wish to be as sustainable as possible. Coffee grounds can also be inexpensive as you can reuse those from your kitchen or enquire about getting free grounds from a local grocery store. Coffee grounds are high in important nutrients like nitrogen, and, thanks to the brewing process, the grounds have already been pasteurized. When preparing coffee grounds to use as a substrate, you will need to add water to the grounds until they have reached the correct moisture content. To increase the air exchange mycelium needs, you can add a small amount of straw to the coffee grounds. Once you begin adding the spawn, use one part of the mushroom spawn for every ten parts of the coffee grounds. Mushrooms that can be grown using a coffee grounds substrate include reishi and shiitake mushrooms.

Hardwood Pellets

Hardwood Pellets/Credit: www.sporeshift.co.nz

You could use virtually any form of hardwood, like beech, oak or maple, as a substrate for a variety of mushrooms. Hardwood pellets are available at most hardwood stores, and you do not need to opt for the more expensive variants like apple or hickory; a bag of oak is perfectly fine. While turning sawdust into pellets, the material is sterilized, so you do not need to sterilize the substrate before use. You need to add 9.5 ounces of water for every cup of pellets. Although not compulsory, many cultivators supplement hardwood pellets with wheat or oat bran. If you add supplements, these materials will need to be sterilized before or after being added to the pellets. You can grow oyster mushrooms, lion's mane, maitake, and reishi on hardwood pellet substrates.

Logs

Logs make for great substrates for mushrooms that are usually cultivated outdoors. As with hardwood pellets, it is wise to stick to hardwood varieties for your logs including elm, birch, poplar, and oak. Ideally, the logs should be between three and four feet long and four and six inches in diameter to allow optimal growth. Avoid using wood that has been lying dead for some time as other fungi may have already settled on the material, making it difficult for the mushroom's mycelium to establish itself. Drill holes that are four to six inches deep into the chosen log in rows, staggering the rows three inches apart and using a 12 mm drill bit. This will allow you to easily insert plug spawn into the log and make it easier for the mycelium to begin colonization. Shiitake and oyster mushrooms can be grown outside on hardwood logs.

Manure

Certain mushrooms grow quite well on substrates like manure and composted manure, but these often need some help as you will need to heat and sterilize these substrates properly. If you are squeamish, there might be better substrate than manure as it will mean regularly working with heated animal feces. Chicken, cow, and horse manure can be used in this substrate. Mix two parts of the chosen material with one part of coco coir and add water until the field capacity has been reached. This means the substrate needs to hold a certain amount of water without extra pooling at the bottom of the growing container. If you give the mixture a hard squeeze, only a few drops of water should escape. Common button mushrooms thrive when grown with manure as a substrate.

Master's Mix

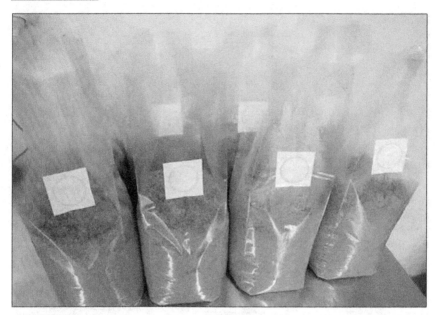

Master's mix/Credit: www.mycologic.nz

Master's mix is a relatively simple substrate to make as it is made up of 50% soybean pellets and 50% hardwood pellets. The medium will need to be sterilized before inoculation. Master's mix is known to be a combination of materials that produce good yields while still being affordable. By good yields, I mean that it is said that this substrate has a larger yield than traditionally expected or than you would get from other substrates. Oyster mushrooms grow particularly well with this substrate.

Straw

Straw/Credit: www.mycologic.nz

The final most commonly used substrate to take note of is straw. Straw is an inexpensive and effective material to create a substrate with. You can use a straw without any supplements or add supplements to provide the mycelium with additional nutrients and resources. The straw substrate can be prepared in various ways including fermenting it for a week or using a heating method. The straw will need to be pasteurized before being inoculated. You will know it is ready for inoculation when only a few drops of water escape the medium when it is given a hard squeeze. You can grow golden oysters, pink oysters, blue oysters, and wine cap mushrooms using a straw-based substrate.

Now that you know which kind of substrates are the best to use in the cultivation process, we can dive into preparing the substrate. Before inoculation, most substrates need to be sterilized or pasteurized. This reduces the chances that other contaminants invade and take over the substrate. But how do you know which technique should be used for which substrate? Well, read on to find out!

Sterilization vs Pasteurization of the Substrate

When you begin preparing your substrate for inoculation, it is important that you know whether the chosen substrate needs to be pasteurized or sterilized and how to go about doing so. Since ideal mushroom substrates are full of nutrition and create an environment conducive to growth, it becomes an environment where other organisms can thrive. Both methods, regardless of which one the substrate requires, are essential to ensuring that the number of potential contaminants is reduced as much as possible. When you take the time to prepare your substrate and protect the mushroom, you limit the possibility of bacterial or other fungal spores invading the substrate and competing with the mushroom's mycelium for nutrients.

The Difference Between Sterilization and Pasteurization

The sterilization process involves heating the substrate until it exceeds 250°F under pressure to eliminate dormant and living contaminants that might have already invaded the substrate. Heating the substrate to these extreme temperatures and applying pressure will create an environment where contaminants cannot grow or function. Simply boiling a substrate will not expose it to a temperature high enough to remove all the contaminants. You will need to use a pressure cooker or equipment equal to one to sterilize the substrate completely. The number of nutrients in the chosen substrate will play a role in determining whether it needs to be sterilized.

However, some substrates need to be pasteurized instead of sterilized. The pasteurization process heats the substrate to a temperature between 150°F and 180°F for no more than two hours. While pasteurizing the substrate does not remove all of the contaminants, it does reduce the number of microbes in the material, giving the mushroom mycelium an advantage and allowing it to push out enemy organisms. Some of the microorganisms that survive the process can eventually benefit mushroom growth.

The main difference between these two processes is that sterilization kills all of the substrate's contaminants. At the same time, pasteurization aims to reduce the number of competing organisms. The type of substrate used, and the nutrient level of the material will determine which method to use.

When to Pasteurize and When to Sterilize

Substrates with a higher nutrient level need to be sterilized instead of pasteurized. Due to the number of nutrients in specific substrates, the material becomes the ideal food source and growing climate for various microbes, resulting in the mushroom mycelium competing with various organisms for food and other nutrients. If the substrate has a lower nutrient count it does not need to be sterilized but should instead be pasteurized. A low-nutrient level indicates that the substrate is not a good food source for contaminants, so the process to eliminate these does not have to be as vigorous as sterilization as it is unlikely that the same number of contaminants will want to invade low-nutrient substrates. However, if you enrich a low-nutrient substrate with supplements it will have to be sterilized as it then becomes a better source of food for other organisms.

Sterilization Methods

There are a few methods of sterilization that can be done at home. Some are more commonly used methods than others, like using a pressure cooker or sterilizing the substrate with hydrogen peroxide. Before we delve into the methods of sterilization, it is important to remember to be safe. When sterilizing substrate you will be working with extreme temperatures that could harm you and a chemical that, if too much is used, could harm the substrate and mushrooms. So, when sterilizing the substrate, work carefully and safely to ensure you are not at risk of being injured.

Sterilizing Substrate with Steam

Autoclave Sterilization/Credit: www.mushroom.guide.com

Also known as steam sterilization, this is one of the most used methods to sterilize substrates. You do not need to use a pressure cooker for this method, but you could use an autoclave, pressure canner, or anything that holds and releases steam. Sawdust-based substrate, or substrate that contains straw, is one of the substrate types that need to be sterilized before the mushroom spawn can be inoculated. Once you have combined the necessary materials and added any supplements, place the substrate mixture in a heat-resistant plastic bag. The tops of the bag need to be folded over so the filter patch can allow gas to escape when the bag is heated. Once the substrate has been placed into the bag and the bag has been properly sealed, adhere to the following steps:

- Before putting your bags or jars into the pressure cooker, ensure that the steam will not enter your bags/jars through the filters. Fold the bags, so the filter is not exposed to air, and cover the jar filters with foil.

- Place your bags/jars on a metal rack to prevent them from touching the bottom of the cooker. Too much heat could cause bags to melt and jars to crack.

- Pour water into your cooker. You need to ensure enough water to last until the end of the process. The water inside doesn't need to dry up completely.

- Close the pressure cooker, put it on a gas cooker or a stove and cook at maximum heat. Set the pressure control to 15 PSI. You can then adjust the stove so that 15 PSI is maintained and not too much vapor spills out of the cooker. Continue cooking the bags/jars for approximately 2 hours.

- Using protective gear like oven mitts, remove the basket from the pressure cooker and the bag from the basket.

- Keep the substrate in an area where contaminants cannot get to it.

- Let it cool to 86°F before inoculating the substrate with the spawn.

This process is relatively easy, and you should have no issues operating the equipment you choose to use. It is also a sterilization method that works on substrates with high nitrogen levels and substrates that have been supplemented. However, this method does consume a lot of energy and purchasing the proper equipment can be quite expensive. Steam sterilization also does not allow for large patches of the substrate to be sterilized at once, and you will need to attend to and monitor the process constantly.

Sterilizing Substrate Using Hydrogen Peroxide

Hydrated Lime/Credit: www.sporeshift.co.nz

When growing mushrooms in a lab or at home, hydrogen peroxide can play a crucial role in creating a sterile environment with ideal growing conditions. Hydrogen peroxide will aid in killing fungal and bacterial spores in the environment that could pose a threat to the mushrooms. These are the steps you need to follow to sterilize the substrate using hydrogen peroxide:

1. Mix the substrate thoroughly with 3% hydrogen peroxide.

2. Place the substrate in a container that can be closed and leave it untouched for 24 hours.

3. Once the 24 hours have passed, drain the substrate and rinse it with clean water.

4. The substrate should now be free of any bacteria or other fungi that might have been present in the substrate.

When using hydrogen peroxide, it is important to work extremely carefully as it is straightforward to damage the mushrooms when not used correctly. Hydrogen peroxide should always be mixed with water and not sprayed directly onto the mushrooms as pure hydrogen peroxide can damage the delicate structures of the fungi. If you use hydrogen peroxide, ensure that the growing environment is not in direct sunlight and is well-ventilated. Direct sunlight and inadequate ventilation can cause the hydrogen peroxide to break down before it can adequately sterilize the substrate.

Tyndallization

With this method of sterilization, the substrate is heat treated in cycles in a process that spans three days or 72 hours. The process consists of three cycles that work as follows:

1. Heat the substrate, through boiling the bag or jar, to 212°F for 30 minutes.

2. Then bring the heat down to 98°F for 12 hours.

3. Once 12 hours have passed, bring the heat back up to 212°F for another 30 minutes.

4. Repeat the second and third steps until 72 hours have passed.

During the second step, which can also be seen as the germination phase, any bacteria in the substrate can begin to grow or cease being dormant. These bacteria are killed during the third step, which is when sterilization takes place. This process is repeated to ensure no harmful bacteria remain. You can expect to repeat these three cycles five or six times over the course of the 72 hours.

Pasteurization Methods

If you are using low-nutrient substrates and do not plan on supplementing the substrate, the process used to eliminate contaminants changes from sterilization to pasteurization. As with sterilization, there are a few methods you can use in order to pasteurize the substrate.

Pasteurizing Substrate Using Hot Water

You can view this method as giving the substrate a hot water bath to get rid of most of the living or dormant microbes present in the substrate. Pasteurizing using hot water is often seen as a DIY method as you either have everything you need or can build some of the things you need. Pasteurization occurs at temperatures between 158°F and 176°F. It can take four to seven hours to pasteurize the substrate and roughly 12 hours to cool down and drain properly.

1. Fill a tub or big container like a barrel with hot water. Use a thermometer to ensure the ideal temperature has been reached.

2. Place the substrate in another container, one that allows for water to drain through.

3. Cover the top of the substrate container with something that will keep the substrate inside the container. You want water to be able to enter the container, but you do not want the substrate to float out.

4. Fill a tub or big container like a barrel with hot water. Use a thermometer to ensure the ideal temperature has been reached.

5. Remove the container, drain the water, and allow the substrate to dry in a sterile area.

Pasteurizing substrates using hot water is relatively inexpensive, especially when you can pasteurize a large amount of substrate at once. In addition, you do not have to monitor the substrate during the process; you can get it started and then leave it unattended until an adequate amount of time has passed. However, there are some disadvantages to this method: you need a lot of space as the containers used are quite big, the entire process can take up to 24 hours, and it can only be used for substrates that are low in nitrogen and have not been supplemented.

Pasteurize Substrate Using Cold Water and Lime

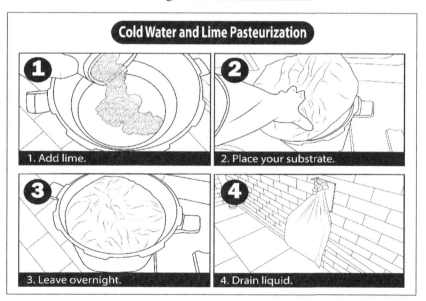

Hydrated lime, or calcium hydroxide, is an organic compound made by superheating lime to bond with extra hydrogen and oxygen atoms. Some cultivators might not consider this method to be pasteurization, as it does not involve heating the substrate. Still, like other methods it eliminates some of the contaminants in the substrate and gives the mycelium a chance to grow. The cold water and lime method is based on mushrooms being better equipped to withstand high pH levels than competing organisms. This pasteurization method works well with dry substrates like wood pellets and bulky material like straw as these can soak up the liquid properly. Remember always to use cold water for this method as hot water will only encourage contaminants to grow.

1. Create a hydrated lime-treated cold-water bath in a container suitable for the amount of substrate and with space for water. You want to use 5g of hydrated lime per liter of water and mix it before it can settle

2. When the lime-treated water has been added, which raises the pH of the water, submerge the substrate in the bath for 24 hours.

3. Once the 24 hours have passed remove the substrate from the bath and drain the excess water

Like the previous method, this one is relatively inexpensive, and you can leave large amounts of substrate unattended for the 24 hours required. Pasteurizing substrate using this method also works well for small batches of the substrate. The disadvantages of this method include not being able to add many supplements to the substrate and that this method only works for faster-growing varieties.

Oven Pasteurization

Pasteurizing your substrate in an oven is one of the simpler methods to eliminate contaminants. In addition to being an easier method, it also requires less cleanup. A disadvantage of this method is that it is less reliable than other pasteurization processes. This is because, compared to hot water, the air is not a great conductor of heat. However, growing mushrooms on a small scale and at home is a good way of keeping them contaminant-free.

You will need the following materials:

- A deep tray, like a turkey tray
- Tin foil
- A thermometer
- A kettle
- Rubber gloves
- The substrate you will be using

Once you have gathered all the items, you can preheat your oven to 400°F and prepare to pasteurize the substrate. These are the steps you need to take:

1. Boil water using the kettle and once done, pour it over the substrate to soak it completely.

2. Let the substrate cool for a few minutes so it is not too hot for you to handle.

3. Put on the rubber gloves and squeeze the water out of the substrate. You want the substrate to be hydrated, but it should not be dripping with water if you press or hold it in your fist.

4. Move the substrate into the tray and cover it with tin foil. If the substrate is fully enclosed, it will keep any water vapor from escaping.

5. Place the tray in your oven and let it "bake" for no less than 30 minutes and no more than one hour.

6. Open the oven and check the temperature of the center of the substrate using your thermostat. If the center of the substrate has reached 180°F you can turn the oven off. If it has not yet reached the desired temperature, leave it in the oven for another 30 minutes.

7. When the center has reached the correct temperature and the oven has been turned off, leave it to cool in the oven for a few hours before removing it. Removing your substrate immediately will allow condensation to form on the inside of the tin foil which will cause problems with hydration.

8. You can remove the substrate when the oven and tray are cooled.

It is best to inoculate your substrate as soon as possible when it has been pasteurized. Waiting to use the substrate can lead to it becoming contaminated and, if this happens, you will need to repeat the entire process.

Additional Pasteurization Methods

Below are two additional pasteurization methods that involve exposing the substrate to a higher temperature thereby eliminating some of the existing contaminants:

- Microwave the substrate in a container for no more than 12 minutes.
- Place substrate in a bag and then place the bag in boiling water for one and a half to two hours.

As this chapter comes to an end, you now know how important properly preparing substrate is to the cultivation process. It is crucial that you take the time to sterilize or pasteurize the substrate to ensure the mushroom mycelium has a chance to colonize the substrate without competing for nutrients. Once the substrate has been prepared, you can begin inoculating it with mushroom spawn, which is exactly what we will tackle in the next chapter.

CHAPTER 9

Inoculation, Incubation, and Fruiting

In this chapter, I guide you through the phase in the cultivation process where you will begin to take more action and see your mushrooms grow. When your chosen spawn and substrate have been prepared, you can begin inoculating the substrate with the mushroom spawn. This process involves introducing the spawn into the substrate, allowing incubation. Once the substrate has been incubated, you might only have to wait a few weeks to see your mushrooms sprout from the growing medium. This chapter will cover the processes of inoculation and incubation in greater detail along with how you should care for your mushrooms during the fruiting phase.

Inoculation

During the inoculation phase it is time to introduce the mushroom spawn to the substrate. It is recommended that this process be completed under sterile conditions to avoid the spawn and substrate being contaminated by mold, bacteria, or other fungi. The importance of keeping a sterile environment has been discussed in a previous chapter but truly comes into play during this phase. If the growing environment, i.e., the substrate, becomes contaminated, your mushrooms will have to compete with other organisms for nutrients and will likely lose the fight.

When the mushroom spawn is brought into contact with the substrate, its growth and development are initiated. From this moment, the mycelium begins to spread, hyphal knots form and eventually fruiting bodies appear above the growing medium. Different substrates follow different inoculation methods; you might have to cut wedges into a stump, drill holes for pegs into a log, or mix spawn into substrate bags. As mentioned above, it is important to keep a sterile environment, but this is mainly a concern when cultivating mushrooms indoors. Outdoor cultivation does not call for a sterile growing environment as outdoor-growing mushrooms are more able to fight off contaminants than indoor-growing mushrooms. Three factors will influence how you approach the inoculation process and the steps you take during this phase: where the process takes place, inoculation rates, and spawn distribution.

Where Inoculation Takes Place

The location where inoculation will be performed depends on the number of nutrients available in the substrate. Substrates like straw, logs, and wood chips generally have low nitrogen levels and are carbon-rich. These substrates can be inoculated outside in the open air. While sterility is not an absolute requirement, it is still wise to keep the operation as clean as possible; keep a clean surface, clean your hands, use clean equipment, and so on. You must maintain a sterile environment if you use substrates with high nitrogen levels like grain and supplemented sawdust. Microorganisms grow quite easily on these kinds of substrates as they are an ideal food source, so your inoculation setting needs to be extremely sterile, almost lab-like, to avoid the substrate being contaminated.

Inoculation Rates

The inoculation rate refers to the amount of spawn mixed or inserted into the substrate. These are a balance between the speed of spawn run and economics. As the cultivator, your concern is to grow healthy mushroom mycelium that will eventually develop the perfect edible mushrooms. A higher inoculation rate indicates that a larger amount of spawn was added to the substrate, and the higher the inoculation rate, the quicker the mycelium can grow through and colonize the substrate. The economic aspect of the balance relates to the inoculation rate, the yield, and the amount of money spent on mushroom spawn. A higher inoculation rate does not often lead to a larger yield, but it does mean that you have spent more money on mushroom spawn per pound of mushrooms.

However, do not be discouraged from creating a high inoculation rate by the financial aspect. If you are a beginner in mushroom cultivation, it's important to remember that a high inoculation rate boosts the success rate of your growth. As you become more familiar and comfortable with the cultivation process, you can then lower the inoculation rate. As the inoculation rate is lowered, you might note a difference in the time it takes for the substrate to be fully colonized. Lower inoculation rates might lead to a longer incubation period which will, in turn, slightly delay the pinning and fruiting phases.

Spawn Distribution

How the spawn is distributed throughout the substrate also impacts how quickly the substrate is colonized. The most used distribution methods are "through spawning" and "top spawning." Through spawning involves shaking the substrate container after inoculation to allow the spawn to become evenly distributed throughout the growing medium. This method of spawn distribution shortens the colonization process but adds a bit of extra physical labor to the process. If you use a lower-tech method like straw tubes and wood chip beds, through spawning is achieved by layering the spawn and substrate much like you would a lasagna. This process of alternating between the spawn and the substrate allows colonization to occur quicker than if you were applying the top spawn method. If you are growing mushrooms outside and using logs, you will likely inoculate these using something like plug and dowel spawn. Dowels are cut to fit holes made in the logs and contain the mycelium of your chosen mushrooms. Once the dowels are plugged into the log, the mycelium can begin to spread.

Top spawning entails only adding spawn on top of the substrate and allowing it to grow down into the substrate. If you use a container that cannot be shaken, like a jar, usually packed tightly, or for low-stakes cultivation, top spawning is the perfect distribution method. Be aware that distribution through top spawning can lengthen the colonization process, which gives contaminants more time to invade the substrate and cease mycelial growth.

Incubation

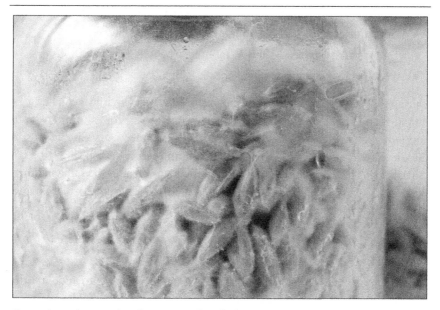

Once the substrate has been inoculated, the spawn requires time to allow the mycelium to leap off onto the substrate and spread throughout the growing medium. You must maintain a sterile environment while the mycelium spreads as you do not want it to compete with bacteria or other fungi before it has had the chance to spread. The leap off, which occurs when the mycelium leaps off the spawn onto the substrate, usually takes place about four days after the substrate has been inoculated. The mycelium spreads through the substrate in a three-dimensional sphere, seeking another leap-off point. Once the two ends meet, the mycelium melds together and continues seeking another leap-off point until the mycelium has colonized the entire substrate. Full colonization occurs once the mycelium has spread in the whole substrate block or container. You can now initiate the mycelium into fruiting.

The rate at which incubation or colonization happens depends on the compactness of the substrate and the mushroom species. For example, a sawdust-based substrate is inoculated much more quickly than logs. When using mushrooms as an example, oyster mushrooms grow faster than shiitake, and the incubation time on various substrates might typically look as follows:

- Oyster logs take between four and twelve months to incubate.
- Oyster mushrooms on sawdust take between 10 and 20 days to incubate.
- Oyster mushrooms on straw take between 14 and 28 days to incubate.

- Shiitake logs take between six and eighteen months to incubate.
- Shiitake on sawdust takes between 42 and 84 days to incubate.
- Specialties on sawdust take roughly 21 days to incubate.
- Stumps take between 24 and 36 months to be fully incubated.
- Wood chips can take up to 12 months to incubate.

During the incubation phase, you want to prioritize two environmental factors: humidity and temperature. You will need to maintain the proper humidity levels and temperature during this incubation phase, as unnecessary fluctuations in these levels may stunt mycelial growth. Lighting and carbon dioxide levels are not crucial to this phase, so you do not need to maintain them in the same manner. Both factors can be adjusted during this phase to suit your comfort level while working. However, different factors need to be considered during the incubation stage when cultivating mushrooms outdoors instead of indoors.

Outdoor Incubation vs Indoor Incubation

When you are cultivating mushrooms outdoors as opposed to indoors, the process of incubation and the factors to consider differ slightly. In the following two sections, we'll take a closer look at the differences in incubation between mushrooms cultivated indoors and outdoors.

Incubation for Mushrooms Cultivated Outdoors

When cultivating mushrooms outdoors, you should prioritize the moisture levels of the mycelium during incubation, i.e., ensure the mycelium does not dry out. If you use logs as the substrate, you will know they need to be soaked in water once the ends begin cracking and you can fit a dime-sized object into the cracks. The logs should be soaked for eight hours to allow the water to seep properly into the log. Typically, the logs cracking, and the subsequent soaking, should not occur more than once a month during the summer. When using wood chips beds as substrate, water the material when inoculating and then once per week for a month. To ensure the bed maintains its moisture, place it in the shade and check that the wood chips are four inches or deeper.

Incubation for Mushrooms Cultivated Indoors

If you are cultivating mushrooms indoors, the incubation phase can create the ideal opportunity for establishing proper space utilization. By working with fluctuating factors such as inoculation rate, strain, substrate, and temperature, you can shorten the incubation time, leading to more mushrooms being produced in the same amount of space. Space is one of many factors in indoor cultivation that differs in importance from outdoor cultivation. Maintaining and monitoring the substrate's water content is not as crucial in indoor incubation because the substrate is kept in a container that does not allow water to escape. When preparing the substrate, you should provide it with the water required to allow the spawn to spread and the mycelium to colonize.

Temperature, however plays a critical role in the incubation phase when cultivating mushrooms indoors. During incubation the ideal temperature is around 70°F and should not exceed 80°F. If you use five or ten-pound bags of supplemented sawdust substrate, the internal temperature of the bag should not be more than 15°F warmer than the exterior temperature. For example, if the temperature outside is 80°F then the core of the substrate can be 95°F. Anything above this level can lead to the mycelium cooking itself, and can also invite contaminants into the substrate. You can regulate the outside temperature to be as low as 50°F but be aware that incubation will take longer to be completed.

When working in a well-insulated room, you will have to focus more on lowering the temperature than raising it as mycelium generates heat while growing. If you do not give your containers ample shelf space, they can easily overheat. Typically, you want a hand's width of space between each growing container because this allows for proper airflow. Areas where containers touch can quickly overheat due to the heat produced by mycelial growth. Overheating can lead to the mycelium dying and allowing contaminants to infiltrate the substrate.

The inoculation and incubation processes can differ depending on the substrate and mushroom species. When walking you through the 10 DIY mushroom-growing projects, we will take a closer look at how inoculation and incubation look when using various substrates to grow mushrooms.

Initiation

Initiation, or pinning, typically indicates the beginning of the fruiting phase. This phase is associated with the tiny mushroom pinheads appearing above the substrate once the growing medium has been fully colonized. This part of the growing cycle links the growth of the mycelium to the eventual formation of the mushrooms. During the pinning phase, you can begin aiding the mycelium in its growing process by initiating fruiting; hence the name of the stage. Unlike plants which take their cues from the environment on when to bloom or fruit, you need to let your mycelium know when it can begin fruiting and aid it in this process.

It is easy to see when the mycelium has fully colonized the substrate. Specifically, because the mycelium is white and rope-like, you should be able to see it moving through the substrate clearly. When there are no more untouched areas, the substrate has been fully colonized and you can begin initiating the fruiting process. In the wilderness, the mycelium will spread as far as it can, absorb the needed nutrients, and begin fruiting naturally. When cultivating mushrooms at home, you will need to take the end of the colonization stage as a natural cue that fruiting bodies can now begin to grow.

There are certain factors that influence the fruiting process and that you can adjust to allow the mycelium to begin pinning.

If you are growing mushrooms in containers, which differ significantly from their natural habitat, lowering the carbon dioxide levels in the growing environment will stimulate the fungus and invite it to begin reaching for the environment outside its container. Most cultivators will punch small holes into the sides to help the pins and mushrooms emerge from the container. As cultivators tend to grow mushrooms in plastic bags, this process is relatively easy and allows the fruiting bodies to reach the environment outside the container. By slightly increasing the light levels, the mycelium will be able to tell that it has reached the surface of the substrate and can begin pushing the fruiting body upwards.

The fungi are likely waiting for a seasonal change, although the shift from one specific season to another depends on the species, before pinning. You can imitate a change in season by increasing the humidity, so the level is close to 100%, and by decreasing or increasing the temperature. Whether you need to lower or raise the temperature depends entirely on which season the mushroom needs it to be. Oyster mushrooms, for example, are divided into cold and warm weather types. Warm-weather oysters can be prompted to fruit by adjusting the temperature to between 50°F and 75°F, while cold-weather mushrooms will begin fruiting in temperatures more in the range of 50°F to 60°F.

By adjusting the growing environment to mimic what mushrooms would naturally experience, you allow the mycelium to create primordia, or hyphal knots, which will soon appear above the substrate's surface. As the pins form, the mushroom employs cell division to form all the cells it will need to produce a mature mushroom. When the pins have formed, it is a matter of giving the mycelium time to stop the cell division and inundate the established cells with nutrients and water, which will prompt them to expand rapidly. Not all the pins will grow into mushrooms; only those with the highest survival likelihood will mature. So, once the pins begin to grow, the mushrooms have entered the fruiting phase.

Fruiting

While pinning forms part of the fruiting stage, some think the fruiting stage begins once the pins start growing. In truth, when incubation is complete, and you begin to change the growing conditions, you have initiated the fruiting phase. As mentioned in the previous section, fruiting is initiated by exposing the colonized substrate to fresh air and lowering the level of carbon dioxide in the growing environment. You want to keep the substrate moist during this phase by misting it with water throughout the day. Though I have briefly mentioned what the ideal fruiting conditions are, it is important to discuss these conditions in more detail.

Creating the Ideal Fruiting Conditions

Once the mycelium is ready to create fruits, you will need to adjust the conditions of the growing environment to encourage the fungi to create pins and, eventually, form mushrooms. The specifications of some of the factors will vary from one mushroom species to another, but the factors that need to change remain the same. These factors include humidity, temperature, light, and carbon dioxide.

Temperature

Mushrooms can endure a range of temperatures, and because of this you should be able to grow mushrooms regardless of the season. If you are not using something like a fruiting chamber to regulate the temperature, the rate at which your mushrooms grow will differ slightly. In colder temperatures, mushrooms will grow slower, and you will likely have a smaller yield. If the temperatures are higher, the mushrooms will grow relatively quickly, but are more open to being contaminated.

Humidity

For mushrooms to fruit, they need to be in an environment with high humidity. You can change the humidity levels of the growing environment in several ways; the method you use will depend on how you have grown your mushrooms up to this point. For example, when growing mushrooms in a bag, you will use a different method to raise the humidity than when you grow mushrooms in a bucket.

Light and Carbon Dioxide

Most mushrooms will require a lower level of carbon dioxide and a higher light level to fruit. The level of carbon dioxide will differ depending on the species, so you must carefully monitor it once the incubation phase reaches its end. You can adjust the light levels by opening some holes in the growing container as this indicates to the mycelium that it can push the pinheads to the surface and begin fruiting.

Home cultivators often opt to use some sort of fruiting chamber to create these ideal conditions. Fruiting chambers are especially helpful for monitoring the conditions of the growing environment. In the following section, we'll take a closer look at the most used fruiting chambers.

Fruiting Chambers and How to Use Them

At this point, you may be wondering what a fruiting chamber is. Essentially, these enclosed spaces create growing conditions that closely mimic natural mushroom growing conditions. There are a variety of fruiting chambers from which you can choose depending on factors like your skill level and space. You can leave your mushrooms to fruit in the container where you have been growing them, but some cultivators prefer to use other methods to help them monitor the conditions more closely. Below are examples of different fruiting chambers you can use, how they work, and how to make them yourself.

Monotubs

Monotub/Credit: www.myshrooms.co.za

Along with Martha grow tents and shotgun fruiting chambers, monotubs are relatively inexpensive and you can make your own at home. These are also one of the most basic and commonly used mushroom fruiting chambers. Monotubs typically resemble or are made of large totes with air holes in the bottom of the sides. Monotubs can hold a great number of mushrooms and are reusable, so once the mushrooms have finished fruiting and have been harvested, you can use the monotub again and fruit other mushrooms.

In short, monotubs are low-maintenance, inexpensive fruiting chambers typically made from totes or large plastic tubs. If you plan to cultivate mushrooms on a small scale, meaning only for personal use, monotubs are an ideal fruiting chamber as they only take up a little space. As a small-scale cultivator, the only disadvantage of monotubs is that they are only suitable fruiting chambers for some mushroom species, so you would need to ensure they are ideal for and can accommodate the mushrooms you are growing. If you are a large-scale mushroom grower, you will find that the monotub is not the best choice for the fruiting chamber for you due to its size and capacity.

You can grow the following mushrooms in a monotub:

- Edible mushrooms that prefer manure as a substrate like button mushrooms or cremini.
- Mushrooms grown on hardwood-based substrate and that fruit from the top of the substrate like wine caps, king oysters and pioppino mushrooms.
- Some side fruiting oyster mushrooms like blue oysters, pearl oysters, phoenix oysters, and pink oysters.
- A medicinal mushroom like reishi can also be grown in a monotub.

Luckily, if you plan on growing any of these mushrooms, you will find it easy to create your own monotub at home. You will need the following:

- A clear plastic bin with a lid. It should be a manageable size
- Opaque plastic bags or black spray paint
- A hand drill with a two-inch hole saw or a utility knife
- Monotub filters, micropore tape of polyfill
- Heavy-duty tape

Once you have gathered all your supplies, you can begin making your monotub. The steps you need to follow are quite easy and, before you know it, you will have a monotub ready to use in the fruiting process.

Step 1: Line or Paint the Container

When encouraging fruiting in a monotub, you will ideally like the pinheads to form on top of the substrate instead of on the bottom or sides of the growing medium. As mentioned, fungi use fresh air and light as a sign to begin producing fruit in the wilderness and because monotubs are clear to allow natural light to seep in, you want to cover the sides and bottom to block out the light. If you neglect to do this, your mushrooms can sprout on all sides of the substrate instead of only on top. You only need to cover a few inches of the tub's sides or as high as the substrate reaches. You can do this by using black spray paint and covering the bottom and sides with paint. Remember to paint the outside of the container, otherwise toxins from the paint could infiltrate and damage your substrate. Alternatively, you can use opaque plastic bags to line the bottom of the tub. If you are going to be using liner, refrain from installing it until right before using the monotub.

Step 2: Make Holes in the Tub

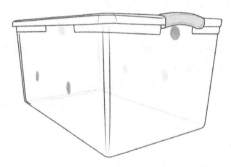

You need to make holes in the monotub to allow air to flow to the mycelium and for the mushrooms to breathe as they grow. Use your drill to make two-inch holes with a hole saw or, if you do not have a drill, cut the holes using a utility knife. If neither of these is available, you can make holes using heavy-duty shears. On the length of each long side of the tub, you should drill a hole every eight inches and there should be one hole on each short side. Drill the holes on the short sides close to the top of the monotub, and those on the long sides just above where the paint or liner ends. Air will flow into the monotub through the lower holes and out through the ones at the top.

Step 3: Fill or Cover the Holes

Besides being an aid in controlling the conditions of the growing environment, fruiting chambers also help combat contamination. Fruiting chambers not only maintain the ideal growing conditions for mushrooms but for other fungi as well. Covering the holes can prevent other bacteria or fungal spores from entering the chamber, invading the substrate, and threatening the mycelium. However, the air still needs to be able to flow through the holes so you will need to use a microfilter, or something similar, to keep the contaminants at bay. You can either fill the holes with Polyfill, cover them with micropore tape, or use adhesive monotub filters to fit the drilled holes perfectly.

Once the holes have been covered or filled, you can use the monotub fruiting chamber. At this point, the monotub is very low-tech, but there are ways in which it can be automated to make maintaining the ideal conditions much easier. A monotub can be automated by adding equipment like a cycle timer, a fan, a humidifier and humidity regulator, and LED lighting. These, however are not essential, and a monotub can be just as useful without these additional materials. Once everything is set up, you can begin growing your mushrooms in the monotub.

To begin growing your mushrooms using this method, you will need the following:

- Mushroom grain spawn
- Bulk substrate
- 70% Isopropyl alcohol
- Two spray bottles
- Latex gloves
- Monotub

Some of these components like the spawn and the substrate, will differ depending on the mushrooms you wish to grow. When you have gathered everything, you will need, you can get started.

Step 1: Clean the Monotub and the Workspace

This step is essential because you want to do everything in your power to eliminate the possibility of contaminants invading the substrate. Ideally, the entire growing process should occur in a room where the doors and windows can be closed and dust is not likely to settle. Fill one of the spray bottles with alcohol and spray any tools you will be using, any surfaces you will be working on, and grain spawn and bulk substrate bags. Remember to wipe the monotub and its lid with alcohol, both outside and inside, and let it dry. Now is also the time to insert the liner in the tub if you are opting to use a liner. Give the liner the same cleaning treatment as the container and its lid.

Step 2: Inoculate the Substrate

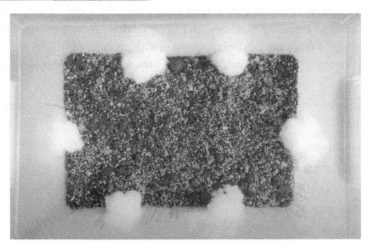

Substrate in Monotub/Credit: www.northspore.com

After cleaning everything, you can move your bulk substrate into the monotub and inoculate it using the chosen spawn. The amount of substrate you place in the tub will depend on its size, but it is usually recommended that you add at least five inches to the container. The amount of spawn you add will depend on various factors, including the type of mushroom, your desired spawn rate, and so on. Before inoculating the substrate, ensure the moisture content is at field capacity. You can check this by lightly squeezing some substrate parts; they should cling together and release a little water. Excess water could lead to a humidity level that is too high for proper inoculation to take place. Therefore you must squeeze the substrate to check the moisture content.

Step 3: Incubation

Once you have introduced the spawn to the substrate and the lid of the monotub has been closed, do not open it during incubation. You want to disturb the substrate as little as possible or not at all. However, do daily checks to see if colonization is progressing. Depending on the mushroom species, you can expect to see fruit begin to form between seven and 25 days. When the entire substrate has been overtaken by mycelium and looks white, and hyphal knots form, you will know that the mushrooms are ready to fruit.

Step 4: The Casing and Fruiting Stage

The moment you see hyphal knots or primordia form, you need to put your monotub into fruiting conditions. Though this step is optional, some cultivators add a thin casing layer of vermiculite or coco coir to the top of the substrate. This helps the mycelium hold knot moisture. While the mushrooms are fruiting, keep the monotub close to a window where it can receive indirect sunlight. No matter how tempting it may be, keep the monotub away from direct sunlight. This can heat the tub and dry out the substrate. In addition to giving it indirect sunlight, try to mist the monotub twice a day—you need to see tiny water droplets on the growing medium's surface.

Once the mycelium has taken over the substrate, mushroom pinheads will form over a few weeks, and you will see them increasing in size almost daily. When your mushrooms have grown significantly, you want to harvest them before fully mature. This will stop them from releasing spores all over your growing area and house. If the species you are growing has a cap, you will want to harvest them before the cap flattens completely as a flat cap is an indication that spores are ready to be released.

Shotgun Fruiting Chambers

Shotgun Fruiting Chamber/Credit: www.cascadiamushroom.com

Shotgun fruiting chambers are similar to monotubs; both are clear totes or containers with holes drilled or carved into the sides. However, there are some differences between monotubs and shotgun fruiting chambers. For example, the method of cultivation used with shotgun fruiting chambers differs from that used with monotubs and shotgun fruiting chambers have more holes than the tubs. As with monotubs, shotgun fruiting chambers can be made at home and aid in creating the ideal environment for your mushrooms to thrive.

This fruiting chamber is low-maintenance and quite easy to put together. It is made of a large, clear plastic container with holes on all sides and a four-inch layer of moist perlite placed at the bottom. It got its name from the scattered and random pattern of holes that resemble bullet holes caused by a shotgun. Shotgun fruiting chambers greatly help first-time cultivators who wish to grow mushrooms like lion's mane, oysters, reishi, and shiitake. These mushrooms are usually grown using plastic bags.

A shotgun fruiting chamber utilizes natural air currents to supply the mycelium with continuous fresh air exchange and maintain humidity. Like monotubs, fresh air goes into the chamber via the bottom holes. However, the process of air leaving the chamber differs slightly due to the container's content. As the air enters the chamber, it moves through the damp perlite which causes the water in the material to evaporate and raise the humidity levels. The humid air that rises to the top of the container then exits through the holes drilled there, allowing fresh air to enter through the bottom once again. In a shotgun fruiting chamber, this constant exchange of fresh air does not lower the humidity levels but helps maintain them.

You can build your own shotgun fruiting chamber at home using the following materials:

- A clear plastic tote, about 70 quarts in size, with a lid. The tote should be tall enough to hold at least four inches of perlite and have 10 inches of space left over for fruiting blocks and growth
- 12 quarts of coarse perlite
- A spray bottle
- Something that will raise the fruiting chamber
- A drill with a quarter inch bit
- A measuring tape
- A marker

When you have gathered all of the supplies, you can begin constructing your shotgun fruiting chamber.

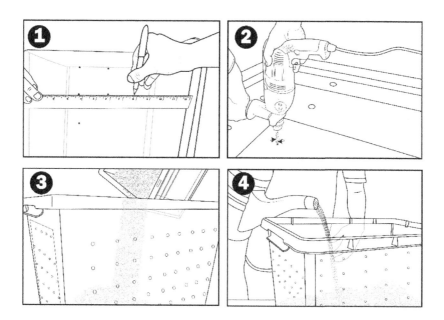

Step 1: Measure and mark where the holes should be

With the measuring tape and marker, carefully mark where the holes need to be drilled into the tote. The holes need to be evenly spaced on all sides of the container, including the lid and bottom of the tote to allow the air to flow properly through the fruiting chamber. The holes should be spaced about two inches apart.

Step 2: Drill the Holes

Once you have marked out where the holes need to be, you can begin drilling them using the quarter inch drill bit. As you do this, work carefully and do not press too hard or you could crack the plastic of the container. Once the holes have been made, remove any loose fragments remaining around the edges of the holes, and wash and dry the container.

Step 3: Add the Perlite

You can now add roughly four inches of coarse perlite to the bottom of the container. You don't have to be too concerned about the depth of this layer, just ensure that you are covering the bottom in an even layer and leave at least five inches of space open above the perlite to allow for proper airflow. Some of the perlite might slip through the holes but this isn't a big concern as it will eventually stop falling through. Using the most coarse perlite you can find will aid in preventing this from happening. Coarse perlite is also beneficial as it has more air compartments to hold water.

Once the perlite layer has been poured into the tote, pour water over it and mix it with a wooden spoon or your hand to disperse the water evenly. You do not want to drench the perlite in water; simply add enough water to moisten the material so it can steadily evaporate and increase the humidity levels in the fruiting chamber.

Step 4: Find a Place to Set Up the Shotgun Fruiting Chamber

It is best to place your shotgun fruiting chamber near a window or other area that receives indirect sunlight and does not experience a draft. If you place the chamber in direct sunlight, you risk drying out the mushrooms and the fruiting chamber can become overheated. Unlike monotubs, you should not run a fan near the chamber because the shotgun fruiting chamber requires airflow but should not be in an extremely drafty area. Though the temperature requirements differ from one mushroom species to the following, many beginner-friendly species will thrive at room temperature.

Step 5: Elevate the Fruiting Chamber

You do not want the shotgun fruiting chamber to be situated directly on a flat surface or its natural currents will not work. It must be elevated slightly and you can do this using legs or a stand. Ideally, you want your shotgun fruiting chamber to be raised at least two inches off the ground, more if possible.

Once you have assembled the fruiting chamber and it has been properly elevated, you can use it to fruit your mushrooms. You will find that a shotgun fruiting chamber is relatively easy to use. Once you have finished building it, you can place the grow bags, kits, or Pf tek cakes inside the container. If you are using Pf tek cakes, you want to place them on pieces of foil so they do not come into direct contact with the perlite. Regardless of what substrate you use, it can be extremely tempting to load the shotgun fruiting chamber full, but overfilling the container will lead to a decrease in airflow, defeating the growing chamber's purpose.

Though a shotgun fruiting chamber is low maintenance, you will still need to put some work into it daily. This is done by spraying and fanning it two times a day. Fanning is when you manually help with air exchange and involves taking off the lid and very lightly fanning the mushrooms twice a day. This allows the stale air at the bottom of the chamber to be replaced with fresh air. After you have fanned the mushrooms, you will have to mist the sides of the container and the perlite to maintain the humidity level. As you spray the perlite and the tote, try to avoid getting water on the mushrooms and substrate as the excess moisture can allow mold to grow.

Martha Grow Tent

A Martha grow tent, or simply a grow tent, is a hybrid of grow tents or greenhouses with humidifiers and can be as simple or as complex as you want it to be. Along with the other fruiting chambers I have mentioned so far, grow tents can also be made at home and customized to suit the available space and the number of mushrooms you wish to grow.

Grow tents can be built in various shapes and sizes and are usually made from a frame covered in canvas, plastic, or reflective sheeting. Martha grow chambers are perfect if you need something bigger than a shotgun fruiting chamber or a monotub, but you do not want to alter a room permanently. These handy tents help you control and maintain the ideal fruiting conditions that your mushrooms require. With a Martha grow tent you can keep these conditions and produce an astonishing number of mushrooms. Martha grow tents are usually medium-sized fruiting chambers and can be used to fruit mushrooms from mediums like blocks, jars, or trays as these tents are often not large enough to fit an entire column bag.

There are a variety of different designs for this fruiting chamber. Here I offer a simpler design that is not too difficult to build at home and is not too complex for beginner cultivators. You will need the following:

- A small greenhouse; a three or four shelf design is perfect
- A dip tray
- Scissors or a knife
- A flathead screwdriver

Once you have gathered all of the materials, you can begin assembling your grow tent.

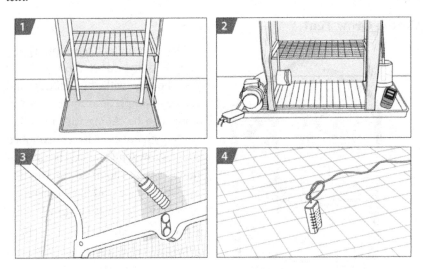

Step 1: Putting the Tent Together

The first step in building a Martha grow tent is to assemble the greenhouse tent. As a beginner, you have likely purchased a brand-new mini greenhouse. If this is the case, it should have instructions that will make assembly much easier. Essentially, you need to put together the outer frame, fit the shelves into their designated spaces, and place the plastic cover over the frame.

Step 2: The Drip Tray

Once you have assembled the mini greenhouse tent you can lift it and place the drip tray underneath. The aim of the drip tray is to prevent any moisture leaving the chamber from damaging your floor.

Step 3: Cut Ventilation Holes

As this is the simpler version of the Martha grow tent and you will not be adding additional equipment, this is the final step in preparing your grow tent. Cut a few small holes in your tent using scissors or a knife to allow air to move through the grow tent. When it is time for the mushrooms to grow and fruit, you can leave the cover's zipper slightly open to aid ventilation. Only create a few holes at this stage; poke only a handful of holes and, if you see the carbon dioxide levels rise at a later stage, you can add a few more. To maintain the ideal humidity levels, add a tray of wet perlite at the bottom level of the grow tent. As with the previous fruiting chambers, keep the Martha grow tent near a window where it can receive some indirect sunlight.

Suppose you wish to automate your Martha grow tent more. In that case, you can add a fan to help maintain proper ventilation and install a humidifier with a sensor that will allow you to monitor and maintain the appropriate humidity levels. You can place an ultrasonic humidifier on the drip tray at the bottom of the grow tent or on the lowest shelf. The sensor I'm referring to is a humidifier controller which is usually placed on the top shelf of the Martha grow tent and helps you monitor the humidity inside the tent. Along with placing the sensor on the top shelf, you can also arrange your fan on the top shelf, ensuring that the exhaust is on the outside of the tent. You can cut a hole into the plastic and push the exhaust through there, but just be sure to cut it so the plastic fits snugly around the fan.

There you have it, everything from inoculating the substrate with spawn to creating fruiting chambers to allow your mushrooms to fruit in ideal conditions. How you approach these phases of the cultivation and growing process depends entirely on variables such as the mushrooms you wish to grow, the substrate you will use, and the amount of space you have available for fruiting chambers. Once you have reached this stage, it is a matter of time before your mushrooms are ready for harvest, which is what I will be discussing in the next chapter.

CHAPTER 10
Harvesting Your Mushrooms

Y ou have finally reached the stage where you can reap the fruits of your labor—literally! Once the mushrooms have created fruit, and before they have matured enough to release their spores, you can harvest and use them either for culinary or medicinal purposes. However, harvesting does not entail simply going around and pulling mushrooms from the substrate. Different mushroom species need to be harvested at different times using different methods. This is precisely what we will be going over in this chapter: how and when to harvest the mushrooms we discussed in "Chapter 5: Choosing Which Mushrooms to Grow".

The Harvesting Process

Harvesting mushrooms is quite easy and you can often harvest all the mushrooms in one flush in one harvesting session. Harvesting becomes a drawn-out process when you have two sets of pins that have sprouted at different stages and are in different growth phases. Not only will the growth stage of the pinheads influence when you can harvest the mushrooms, but the method of cultivation used will also affect the time spent harvesting. If you grow mushrooms using a grow kit, you will find the instructions offer a rough estimate of the perfect time to harvest the mushrooms. If you decide to grow mushrooms from premade spawn or use your own spawn, you will have to monitor the mushrooms more closely to determine the ideal harvest time.

Other factors will also influence when you harvest the fruit, including the conditions in which they have been grown. Any changes in the growing environment might lead to the mushrooms fruiting and being ready for harvest earlier or later than planned. In addition to this, it is important to remember that the size of the mushrooms does not serve as an adequate indicator that they are ready to harvest. A certain species might just naturally be bigger in size, but it does not mean the mushrooms are ready for harvest. Overall, it is better to harvest the mushrooms if their caps have flattened out or are turned upwards instead of downwards.

From the moment the pinheads start to show, most mushrooms should be ready for harvest in one to two weeks, depending on the species. You will see the mushrooms double in size before being ready to harvest but remember not to take this as an absolute. Ideally, except for pinheads, you will want to simultaneously harvest all of the mushrooms in different stages of growth in a flush. Leaving mushrooms smaller than the others might only lead to the mushroom dying or attracting contaminants. You want a good yield, but you also do not want the mushrooms to mature fully, or they could release spores, which will fill your house and could land on substrates meant for other mushrooms.

In the following section, we will look at the perfect time to harvest the mushroom types mentioned earlier in the book. Some of these might be ready for harvest simultaneously, while others will need more time to form fully. I will also give you some tips on how to harvest the mushrooms to avoid damaging them and allow you to make the most of the entire flush. So, without further ado, let's jump into harvesting our mushrooms.

Reishi

When it comes to harvesting reishi mushrooms, it is best to examine the underside of the mushroom to determine whether they are ready. After inoculating the substrate with reishi spawn, it can take about eight weeks for your mushrooms to be ready for harvest. If the reishi is white underneath, it is a young mushroom and will provide you with the most medicinal benefits. Darker colors suggest that it is an older mushroom and, though these can still be harvested, will be more bitter and tough. Older reishi mushrooms can also often contain harmful mold, so it is best to harvest them when they are young. It is wise to note that reishi has a lot of spores, more than some other mushrooms like white buttons, so it is ideal harvesting them before the spores can be released.

When growing reishi on logs or stumps, you can simply pull the mushroom off the tree. Twisting slightly while you pull will help loosen the mushroom. When harvesting younger, softer reishi, you can use a knife to cut them from the tree gently. If you are growing reishi mushrooms using a fruiting block, you can use a serrated knife or sharp blade to cut the mature mushrooms from the block. However, you will have to be careful and work gently so as not to bruise the younger mushrooms that are still growing.

Oyster Mushrooms

As in Chapter 5, we will now take a closer look at the varieties of oyster mushrooms you can choose to grow. The ways in which these are harvested are often quite similar as they are the same species, but their harvest time can differ and, depending on their size, you might need to use a different method. Unless stated otherwise, you can assume that all oyster mushrooms are harvested similarly. While you can cut the oyster mushroom from the substrate, you risk damaging the flush or bruising those not yet ready for harvest. When it comes to oyster mushrooms, it is often best to pull them off by hand. Gently twist and pull the oyster mushrooms off at the base of the stem. You will need to pull the cluster off as one, so work carefully or get someone to help you to avoid damaging or bruising the mushrooms.

Pearl Oyster

As with all other mushrooms grown at home, it is best to harvest pearl oysters before they have fully opened to avoid having spores everywhere. In addition, it is also best to wear a respirator when harvesting these mushrooms because otherwise you may accidentally inhale spores. The proper time to harvest pearl oysters is not determined by their size but by the shape of the cap. The caps should have begun to unfurl and flatten but should not be flat yet. The edges of the caps should still curl slightly when harvesting. Pearl oyster mushrooms should be ready for harvest about five days after the pins begin to form.

Blue Oyster

You will want to harvest your blue oyster mushrooms once the biggest mushrooms in the flush flatten and unfurl their caps. Typically, this happens six to ten days after pinheads have begun to show. Remember, that as oyster mushrooms grow incredibly quickly, you might miss the ideal harvest time by just a matter of hours. Once the pins begin to develop into whole mushrooms, checking your blue oyster regularly is best. If you are worried about harvesting them after they have matured and begun to release spores, it is always better to harvest them a bit earlier. There is no harm in using a younger mushroom and you will not have to worry about spores spreading all over your house.

Phoenix Oyster

As these mushrooms are most commonly grown on logs, you will need to wait longer to harvest them than with pearl or blue oysters. Phoenix oysters fruit between four and twelve months after being inoculated. If the temperature is right, they will fruit anytime from the start of spring to fall and are likely to appear after heavy rain. Of course, when growing these mushrooms at home, you can start the fruiting process at your convenience if the mycelium allows it. Once they have begun fruiting, you will see them grow quite rapidly. Phoenix oyster mushrooms should be ready to be harvested a week after they have started fruiting. The edges of the caps should still be curled down when you are harvesting these mushrooms; if they have begun to flatten you might be harvesting them a tad too late. To harvest phoenix oysters, gently hold the flush at the base and carefully twist the mushrooms off the log.

Pink Oyster

Pink oyster mushrooms can be harvested when their caps begin to curl upwards. Once again, harvesting these before they release their spores is incredibly important. Compared to other oyster mushrooms, pink oysters produce an incredible number of spores - like reishi. If you wait to harvest the mushrooms after they have fully matured, you will have to clean pink spores from every room in your house and risk breathing in them. The fruiting phase usually takes up to 12 days, so you should monitor your pink oysters closely and harvest them as soon as they are ready. Typically, you can expect your mushrooms to be ready for harvest five days after the pins have formed. Pink oyster mushrooms produce multiple flushes, and you can expect to harvest the second flush roughly seven days after your first harvest. Harvest your pink oyster mushrooms by gently twisting and pulling at the base of the flush. As you do this, be careful not to put too much force on other parts of the mushroom as this can lead to bruising.

Golden Oyster

You will have to be extremely careful when harvesting golden mushrooms as their caps are incredibly fragile and can easily be damaged while being harvested. As is typical with oyster mushrooms, golden oysters grow incredibly quickly and are often ready to be harvested between five and ten days after pins form. If you are not keeping track of the number of days that have passed, you can use the size of the mushrooms as a sign that they are ready to be harvested. When golden oyster mushrooms no longer double in size daily and their cap edges flatten slightly, they are ready for harvest. Due to the fragility of the mushroom, it is best to harvest golden oysters using a knife as this lowers the chances of accidentally bruising or breaking their caps and stems. Using a sharp knife, you can remove an entire cluster by cutting at the base of the mushrooms.

King Oyster

Harvesting king oyster mushrooms is a bit different than harvesting other oyster mushrooms. You can decide when you would like to harvest your king oysters as they carry the same nutrients and benefits as young, small mushrooms as they do when mature. King oyster mushrooms are typically ready to be harvested around two weeks after pins have begun to form. When harvesting king oysters, you can either use a sharp knife to cut the mushrooms near the base or you can harvest them by twisting and pulling.

Shiitake Mushrooms

Ideally, you will want to harvest your shiitake mushrooms when 80% of the gills have been exposed and the edges of the caps are curling under. You can also harvest shiitake at any time during the fruiting stage even if they are still somewhat small. If the partial veil has broken and the gills have been exposed, the mushrooms are ready for harvest. If the younger shiitake mushrooms still have intact partial veils, leave them to continue to mature. If your mushrooms' gills have begun to turn brown before harvesting them, it is best not to consume these. It is best to harvest shiitake mushrooms using a sharp knife. Cut them as close as possible to the log or substrate block. In this case, you want to be even more careful not to damage the substrate as shiitake mushrooms produce several flushes and a damaged substrate can hurt future growth.

Lion's Mane Mushrooms

You can prepare to harvest your lion's mane mushrooms between four and seven days after initiation. Size-wise, you will want to harvest lion's mane when they are fist-sized and have elongated, well-defined teeth and spines. The spines of lion's mane mushrooms often grow to be an inch long, but most experienced cultivators suggest harvesting the mushrooms when their spines measure 0.25 inches in length. You could also use their color as an indicator of when to harvest. Harvesting lion's mane mushrooms before they turn into a pinkish or brown color is best. Lion's mane mushrooms are one species that benefit from the twisting and pulling harvesting method. It can be difficult to get a knife close to the base of the mushroom, so it is best to twist and pull them from the substrate gently. If the mushrooms are ready to be harvested, they will pull away from the substrate quite easily.

Cordyceps Mushrooms

Cordyceps mushrooms are a species of mushroom that can take a while to reach the harvest stage. Depending on the variety, it can take a month for the mushroom to mature enough to be ready for harvest. You will know the cordyceps are ready to be harvested when they have stopped growing or reached the maximum height of the growing container. When your cordyceps are ready to be harvested, you can simply grip them at the base and break them off.

White Button Mushrooms

It can take a month after incubation for your white button mushrooms to begin pinning and maturing but harvesting them is incredibly easy once they have reached that stage. The caps of white button mushrooms pop open when they are mature and ready to be harvested. Simply twist at the base and pull them from the substrate. If you do not want to twist the mushrooms for fear of harming them, white button mushrooms can just as easily be harvested with a knife. By using a sharp knife, you can cut through the stem right below where it meets the cap.

What to do With the Used Substrate

Once you have harvested your mushrooms, you end up with what is often referred to as "spent" substrate, i.e., a substrate that has been fully colonized and produced mushrooms. You do not have to completely throw away the substrate as there are several uses for the spent substrate. The most used method of the repurposing substrate is to simply compost it. You can mix it with your existing compost pile or create one only meant for the substrate. Compost piles that consist solely of used substrate break down over time and become rich compost. Sometimes, depending on the substrate and mushroom species, you can get more than one flush from the substrate. You can use the spent substrate to inoculate a new substrate batch. This method can save money because you do not have to buy mushroom spawn or grow kits.

You have harvested your mushrooms and planned to convert your used substrate into compost. Now, what do you do with the mushrooms you have harvested? Well, you can either use them as you please immediately or you can store them for future use. In the next chapter we'll take a closer look at the various ways you can store your mushrooms, like drying or freezing them, and how to get them ready for use quickly. You do not want perfectly good mushrooms to grow to waste or consume poorly prepared mushrooms. This final step in the cultivation process is just as crucial as all the others, so let's get into storing and preparing your freshly harvested mushrooms.

CHAPTER 11
Storing and Preparing the Harvested Mushrooms

Storing your mushrooms and preparing them properly is a crucial step in the process of growing mushrooms. Some mushroom species produce rather large yields, and you will only be able to use them some at a time - even if you have a large family and many friends. The solution is storing your mushrooms so you can properly enjoy them at a later date. There are several ways to store your mushrooms depending on what you plan to use them for, how long they need to be stored, and so on. In addition to adequately storing your mushrooms, you need to know how to prepare them for storing and cooking. In this chapter, I will be explaining to you how to prepare and store your mushrooms properly so you have access to healthy harvests of mushrooms whenever you need them.

Storing Mushrooms

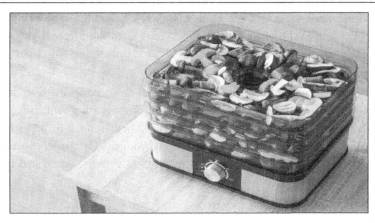

Mushroom Dehydrator

You might think storing mushrooms is as easy as simply placing them in the fridge and using them within a few days. While this is true in some situations, you might want to save mushrooms for more than a few days or use them for medicinal purposes. Your reasons for wanting to store the mushrooms will influence how they should be stored. In this section, we'll look at the various ways in which you can store your mushrooms and keep them ready for use.

Storing Mushrooms in the Fridge

Because a refrigerator is a cold place, you need to store your mushrooms in ways that will not introduce them to excess moisture. Ideally, you want to use a container that will absorb the moisture and keep it away from your mushrooms. Excess moisture can lead to mold developing on your mushrooms and you will find yourself losing more mushrooms than you can produce. There are several ways to store your mushrooms in the refrigerator:

- Keep unwashed whole mushrooms in a brown paper bag with the top folded over in the fridge's main compartment. The bag will absorb additional moisture and keep your mushrooms from developing mold or becoming soggy.

- Place your mushrooms in a glass or plastic container that can be covered with plastic wrap. Poke a few holes in the plastic wrap and store the mushrooms in the fridge. Making holes in the plastic before storing allows the excess moisture to escape and, once in the fridge, it will prevent the mushrooms from drying out. However, with this method moisture can collect at the bottom of the container, so do not store mushrooms for longer than five days using this method.

- You can also store your mushrooms in cardboard punnets. These can keep mushrooms fresh for a good time as they absorb additional moisture while still being a breathable container and keep mushrooms from drying out. If the punnet does not have a cardboard lid, simply slide it into a paper bag and keep it in the fridge.

- The final method involves wrapping your mushrooms in paper towels. Once wrapped, you can place the mushrooms in plastic bags, glass containers, or brown paper bags. Mushrooms wrapped in paper towels and placed in paper bags tend to last longer. The paper towels are breathable while also absorbing any additional moisture created by the cold environment.

In addition to keeping your mushrooms in the proper containers, there are a few other tricks you can use to keep your mushrooms as fresh as possible for as long as possible.

- Avoid storing the mushrooms in a drawer as this area can often be too moist for mushrooms to handle.
- Do not stack other foods on top of the mushrooms. This can bruise and damage the mushrooms, which lowers their shelf life by a few days.
- Keep the mushrooms away from foods that have strong flavors or odors as they tend to absorb these and lose their own distinct flavor.
- If you do not plan on using your mushrooms within a week, consider using a different storing method like drying or freezing.

Freezing Mushrooms

While mushrooms handle extremely cold temperatures well, it is best to freeze them when they are still fresh. Do not wait until the mushrooms begin declining in the fridge before freezing them. Instead, freeze them as soon as possible after you harvest them. If your mushrooms have produced a large yield, you might want to set a few aside and store them in the fridge while freezing the bulk of the yield. Mushrooms can be frozen and kept in the freezer for up to twelve months. You can freeze raw mushrooms, but it is recommended that you steam them before freezing.

Frozen raw mushrooms can lose their texture and become very soft once thawed. In addition, raw mushrooms have a very high-water content that will make the mushrooms soggy when thawed. So, to preserve their taste and texture, it is best to cook them and let them cool completely before placing them in airtight containers and freezing them. To properly maintain the integrity, flavor, and freshness of your mushrooms, spread them apart on a baking tray (or something similar) and put them uncovered in the freezer for 30 minutes. This will keep the mushrooms from sticking together. Once 30 minutes have passed, you can place your mushrooms in airtight containers such as plastic containers or freezer-safe plastic bags.

Drying Mushrooms

If you have limited storage space in your fridge or freezer, you can dry your mushrooms. The good thing about dried mushrooms is that they can be rehydrated and used when needed, and they only take up a little space in your pantry or food storage space. You only need an oven or a food dehydrator to dry mushrooms and an airtight container to store them. If this is your first time drying mushrooms, start with a small batch and learn how to use and reconstitute them before fully committing to using this process. When you have mastered rehydrating mushrooms, you will find that they work just as well in cooking as fresh mushrooms. There are several ways to dry mushrooms, including using an oven, an electric dehydrator, or through air drying.

Oven Drying

1. Preheat your oven to 300°F.
2. While the oven is heating, slice the mushrooms into small pieces and lay them out on a baking tray in a single layer.
3. In total, you want to bake the mushrooms for one hour before flipping them and then baking for another hour. As they are baking, you will need to regularly dab away any moisture that the mushrooms sweat out until they are completely dry.
4. Once two hours have passed, let them cool down completely and store them in an airtight container in a dark, cool place.

Air Drying

Air drying is a drying method that takes longer than the others mentioned but it does conserve a lot of energy, making it the more environmentally-friendly option. When air-drying mushrooms, you need a container that allows air to flow through, like a colander. Place the chosen mushrooms in the container and leave them to dry out for a week; remember that some mushrooms will dry out quickly while others might need a few more days. You will know the mushrooms have dried out completely when they are dry to the touch and do not give up when you squeeze them. The mushrooms should feel a bit like tiny rocks when dried out completely. When they have reached the desired stage, you can store them in an airtight container in a cool dry place for at least two years.

A Food Dehydrator

Many mushroom enjoyers, whether cultivators or foragers, consider food dehydrators one of the best equipment to use when drying mushrooms. It is quite easy to use a dehydrator and you will see the results fairly quickly. It also gives you more control over the airflow and the temperature. In addition, dehydrators don't take up too much space in your house. Once again, you slice the mushrooms into small, thin pieces and place them on the trays. Once you have spaced the mushrooms out in a single layer, place the trays into the dehydrator. Most food dehydrators will have an instruction manual that will guide you through the process and let you know how long you need to keep your mushrooms in the dehydrator. Below is a step-by-step process to dry your mushrooms using a dehydrator.

1. Clean the mushrooms properly before drying them. This entails cleaning off any debris, dirt or small insects that may be hiding on the gills or stems and trimming off the bruised or damaged parts of the mushrooms. If you are growing mushrooms indoors, you will likely not find insects hiding anywhere. However, if you are growing mushrooms outdoors you need to check for insects. You can give them a quick rinse when drying mushrooms, as any additional moisture absorbed will be removed anyway. Pat the mushrooms dry before moving them to the dehydrator.

2. Though it is generally better to slice mushrooms before drying them, smaller mushroom species can be dried whole. Cut the mushrooms into thin slices, preferably 0.4 inches thick. If to grind the mushrooms into powder once dry, you can cut them into small pieces that will make them easier to grind. Try to keep the mushroom pieces all the same thickness and size to avoid some drying more quickly than others.

3. Whether drying whole or sliced mushrooms, you can now arrange them in a single layer on the dehydrator trays while leaving enough space between each slice or mushroom for proper air circulation. Pat down the mushrooms before putting the trays into the dehydrator.

4. Set the dehydrator to a low setting, between 110°F and 135°F, and dry your mushrooms until they are brittle. It typically takes six to eight hours for mushrooms to be dried thoroughly. Check on the mushrooms around the fourth hour as smaller mushrooms or slices can dry quicker while larger mushrooms can take up to 12 hours to be simply dehydrated.

You will know that the mushrooms have dried completely when they are brittle and can be broken relatively easily. This can be tested by allowing the mushrooms to cool and become slightly crispy, then breaking a few pieces. Mushrooms that break easily have been fully dried and those that bend without snapping need a few more hours in the dehydrator.

And so, we have come to the end of mushroom cultivation. You will now be able to create your own small-scale mushroom farm at home. But rest assured; this is not the end of the book! In the next chapter, we will take a closer look at the entire process of making your own spawn. Though this process might seem complicated, it will benefit you in the long run. For now, you can safely say you know exactly how to store and properly prepare your mushrooms for use.

CHAPTER 12
Making Your Own Spawn

In "Chapter 7: Preparing the Mushroom Spawn," I introduced you to two methods of obtaining mushroom spawn: using a grow kit and buying premade spawn. In that chapter, I briefly referred to the process of making your own spawn. This chapter will examine the entire process of creating your own mushroom spawn at home. It is important to note that this process can seem complicated and intimidating, especially if you are a beginner cultivator. Worry not; with this book by your side, you can make your own spawn without fear. It will take some trial and error, but you will soon be able to reap the benefits of creating your own mushroom spawn at home.

Getting to Know Agar

Petri Dishes with Agar/Credit: www.gluckspilze.com

When making your own mushroom spawn at home, you may follow the steps of many other cultivators and use agar. You might have heard about people using agar to generate and transfer mushroom mycelium but have yet to learn what it is or how to use it. In this section we are going to cover everything you need to know about using agar in the process of producing mushroom spawn.

What is Agar?

In short, agar is a setting agent often used in Asian desserts and is made from red algae. Agar is a medium used for mushroom growing, often specifically used to watch mycelium develop, and is made by combining certain materials. The mixture combines nutrients, water, and dried agar, which is obtained from red algae. The materials are mixed and dissolved in hot water, after which it is pressure sterilized and poured into Petri dishes. The agar cools in the petri dish and solidifies into a jelly-like medium on which you can easily observe how spores germinate and mycelium grows. Petri dishes that contain agar are ideal environments for growing several different bacteria and fungi. In the cultivation process, agar often simply refers to a "culture medium;" a substrate filled with nutrients and vitamins needed to grow microorganisms.

Why Use Agar?

When cultivating mushrooms, agar can create monocultures and store cultures for longer without fear of contamination. If you are growing mushrooms at home, especially if you do not have designated sterile lab space, germinating spores on agar before using them can save your mushrooms from contamination. Mushroom spores are often escorted by spores of other fungi or bacteria which means the spawn can easily be contaminated if you do not take the necessary precautions. Using agar plates to cultivate the mycelium allows you to identify the unwanted contaminants visually and makes it easier to transfer clean, uncontaminated mycelium to a new Petri dish.

Obtaining Agar

You can buy agar plates, Petri dishes with agar already set inside them, or make your own. As a beginner you might find it easier to buy your agar plates when first attempting to produce your own mycelium. Many mushroom suppliers, those that sell premade spawn or places that sell grow-kits, will also have agar plates that you can buy. If you decide you would rather make your own agar plates, you might find that this can become quite costly as you will need to purchase the materials with which to make the agar along with Petri dishes and equipment that aids in sterilizing the agar before use.

Transferring Agar from One Petri Dish to Another

Using agar plates to create mushroom mycelium is an excellent way to catch and avoid contaminants early on. You can further minimize the chances of your spawn contamination by transferring the mycelium from one Petri dish to another. There are other reasons why you might wish to transfer agar from one Petri dish to another. For instance, you might want to transfer the culture to keep the mycelium of a certain mushroom species alive indefinitely or you might complete this process simply to verify the purity of your mycelium.

Transferring Cultures from One Agar Plate to Another

While the process of transferring agar can seem daunting when you first try it, with time the process becomes easier. Below, I will be breaking down the entire transferring process into steps that are quite easy to follow.

In order to transfer culture on agar you will need the following:

- Agar plates that are nutrient rich and have been properly prepared
- A scalpel
- A flame or alcohol burner
- A SAB, flow hood or generally sterile environment
- Masking tape
- Mushroom culture on another petri dish

Step 1: Cleaning

Before doing anything else with the agar plates or Petri dishes, clean the dishes you have with rubbing alcohol. You can use this time to clean your other tools, especially the scalpel. Make sure that your hands are as clean as possible. If you are worried about the cleanliness of your hands, you can purchase nitrile gloves and a surgical mask. This will aid in preventing contaminants from moving from your hands or breath to a fresh plate.

Step 2: Get the Dishes Ready

Remove any masking tape already on the Petri dishes—it is usually used to seal the edges. Arrange the dishes to be side by side in front of the flow hood or SAB, whichever you choose to use. You might find it easier to set the new plate on the side of your non-dominant hand and keep the plate you will be cutting closer to your dominant hand.

Step 3: Sterilize the Scalpel

Sterilize your scalpel using a steady flame or an alcohol burner. You will know the scalpel has been properly sterilized when the blade glows red hot. This process must be repeated between every transfer, so you need to have a constant flame ready to go in your work area. The easiest way to have a constant flame is by using an alcohol lamp but if you do not have access to one you could also fill ¾ of a shot glass with rubbing alcohol and set this alight. If you use the latter technique, just be extra careful not to knock the glass over while it is burning.

Step 4: Cool the Blade

When the blade has become red hot, cool it as quickly as possible by dipping it into the agar in the dish that will receive the culture. Carefully lift the lid off the dish and keep your hand on the back half of the lid, away from the rest of the plate. As you do this, avoid contacting the edge of the plate you are holding. Try to handle the plate as little as possible and do not, under any circumstances, remove the lid from the stream of the laminar flow hood or the SAB. Once the lid is removed, quickly set the blade into the agar close to the edge of the dish. You should hear it sizzle quite audibly. As quickly as you can, remove the blade and put the lid back onto the dish.

Step 5: Transfer the Agar

Using the blade that has now been cooled down, open the dish that contains the culture you wish to transfer. Hold the dish as steady as possible while cutting a small piece of agar, preferably one that contains mycelium, from the dish. The piece does not have to be more than 0.39 x 0.39 inches. When you have cut the piece, stab it with the scalpel and speedily transfer it to the receiving dish. You need to place the cut piece in the center of the receiving dish. While doing all of this, constantly keep the culture piece inside the SAB, upstream of the plates if possible.

Step 6: Seal the Plate's Edge

You can now use masking tape to seal the edge of the new plate. Label the dish with the species and the date this process was completed. Once this has been done, move the petri dish to a clean, room-temperature area. You can repeat this process as often as you wish to create more plates.

Now that you have been properly introduced to the wonder that is agar, and you will be able to transfer cultures from one dish to another safely, we can begin delving into the process of making your own spawn. Some methods will allow you to decide if you want to work with agar throughout this process. In the end, the choice is up to you but do keep in mind that utilizing agar can mitigate the chances of your spawn being contaminated.

Methods for Producing Spawn

In this chapter section, we will look at two different methods you can use to create your own spawn at home. The first method involves spore prints to make spawn and the second entails producing spawn using stem butts. I will guide you through both methods step-by-step and include instructions on creating spawn with and without agar using both methods. Let's jump straight into the first method!

Method 1: Producing Spawn from Spore Prints

One way to make your own mushroom spawn is to make spore prints. Making a spore print is relatively easy and you do not need a lot of expensive equipment. But to make a spore print, you should first become familiar with what a spore print is. Mushroom spore prints are patterns made on flat surfaces, like glass or paper, and consist of thousands of spores that have been dropped from the spore-bearing surface. Each mushroom species has spores in various colors, shapes, and sizes. In addition, mushrooms also release spores in interesting and unique patterns. The patterns match the spore-bearing surface that you can see on the underside of the mushroom cap and include the textures of structures like gills, pores, or tubes in which the spores are held before being released.

Making a Mushroom Spore Print

The process of making a spore print is quite easy and simply involves allowing a mature mushroom to drop its spores on a flat surface. You should be able to complete the entire process in no more than five steps.

To make mushroom spore prints, you will need the following:

- A freshly harvested mushroom
- A glass, paper or tin foil surface
- A bowl or glass
- An airtight storage bag

Step 1: Select a Mushroom

To produce the best possible spore print, you want to choose the best possible mushroom. Pick mature mushrooms as these have enough spores to make a distinct print. Younger mushrooms do not have enough spores for a proper spore print and might even still have a partial veil covering the gills. Unless making prints for art or creative purposes, it is best to use flat mushrooms. In addition, choose mushrooms that do not have anything obstructing the spore-bearing surface. Check that no part of the cap, stem, or partial veil is covering the surface. The ideal mushroom should have the following characteristics:

- A fully opened cap and gills or pores that are completely exposed
- Healthy and firm gills or pores that are not wet and soft
- It has to be slightly moist as dry mushrooms do not work well
- The mushroom should not have any bruising, insect damage, or moldy spots

Step 2: Remove the Stem

If the mushroom has a stem attached to the cap, you must carefully separate the stem from the cap. The stems of some mushroom species can easily be snapped off, but it is best to use a scalpel or sharp knife to remove the stem; this will limit any possible damage to the underside of the cap. If you want to make a print of a shelf mushroom, like oyster mushrooms, you can use the entire fruiting body. Because you will be making the print for cultivation purposes, you must keep the work environment clean from this step onwards. This entails ensuring all your tools and hands are as clean as possible and using a sterilized scalpel or knife to remove the stem. Many cultivators prefer to also wipe down the topside of the mushroom cap with isopropyl alcohol which can minimize the opportunity for contaminants to settle on the mushroom.

Step 3: Position the Mushroom Cap

You will need to leave the mushroom undisturbed for 24 hours to produce a proper spore print, so you will need to find a suitable, sterile area. Place the mushroom caps face down on your chosen flat surface; the gills or pores must touch the surface. For our purposes, it is best to use tin foil as this will make it easier to transfer the print later. Clean the tin foil with alcohol before placing the mushroom down to prevent contamination.

Step 4: Cover the Mushroom and Wait

For the best results, you need the spores to fall directly downwards from the cap, so you need to cover the cap with a bowl or glass to keep air currents from shifting or blowing the spores away as they fall. If you are using a larger mushroom to make the spore print, covering it with a bowl or glass will also keep it from drying out. Freshly harvested, mature mushrooms can produce a complete spore print in under two hours. However, some species can take a few more hours or a day to release their spores, so it is best to leave the cap undisturbed for 12 hours.

Once 12 hours have passed, you can carefully move the container from the mushroom cap and gently lift the cap. You should see a pattern on the tin foil that matches the pattern underneath the mushroom cap. The mushroom is either too dry or needs more time if there is no discernible pattern. Place the mushroom back onto the tin foil and cover it for 12 more hours. If the mushroom has made a distinct pattern, you can use the cap to make a few more spore prints. Simply move it to another flat surface or use the same surface and place the mushroom on a different area.

Step 5: Store the Spore Print

Fold the tin foil over so the print is on the inside and place it in a zip-lock bag. Do not move the tin foil with your hands; rather, use tweezers or something similar to transport the spore print. Store the prints in a dark area at room temperature until you wish to transfer them. Spore prints can be kept in these conditions for decades before being used. Once you are ready to use the spore prints, you can either transfer them to agar or use them to make spore syringes.

Transferring Spore Prints to Agar

When you have made all the mushroom spore prints you want and you are ready to begin the cultivation process, you can begin to transfer the spore prints to agar. This process may seem complicated, and there is certainly a learning curve to it. Still, by taking your time and following each step you can successfully inoculate agar and begin your mushroom-growing journey.

To transfer the spore print to agar, you will need the following materials:

- A spore print you have made
- Nutrient rich agar plates (agar set in Petri dishes)
- A needle holder with inoculation loop or a one-way inoculation loop
- Parafilm
- A hairnet and facemask
- Latex gloves
- Spiritus lamp (only if you are using a metal inoculation loop)
- A sterile workspace like a SAB or flow hood
- Workspace and hand disinfectant

To lower the risk of contaminants invading the agar medium, it is best to work in a sterile environment like a laminar flow hood or a SAB. You can take the following steps to minimize the risk of contamination even further:

1. Clean the workspace thoroughly
2. Wash your forearms and hands
3. Put on a face mask, hairnet and latex gloves
4. Disinfect your worktop. You can do this with rubbing alcohol but be sure to allow it to dry completely before starting
5. Disinfect your hands and allow them to dry completely before beginning the transfer.

If you are using a reusable inoculation loop, you can heat it using an alcohol lamp until it is red hot. Once it has reached the appropriate temperature, let it cool down in your hand. The gloves should protect you from the heat but refrain from gripping the inoculation loop or you might be burned. Once everything has been cleaned and sterilized, you can begin the process of transferring spores to the agar medium. However, it is important to remember you must touch the spore print, inoculation loop, and agar medium as little as possible throughout this process. This means only working with the bits of tin foil that do not have the spore print on them, taking care not to touch the agar medium in the Petri dish, and only touching the handle of the inoculation loop and not the loop itself.

Step 1: Gathering Spores

Before beginning to gather spores, gently rub the tip of the inoculation loop on the surface of the agar to collect some moisture that the spores can stick to. Using the inoculation loop, rub the spore print until the loop has gathered a layer of spores. Do not rub the inoculation loop over the entire spore print; pick a section and collect only the spores from that area.

Step 2: Scraping the Spores

Once you have gathered enough spores on the inoculation loop, you can import them onto the agar. Carefully open the Petri dish and avoid touching any part of it except the top of the lid. Scrape the spores onto the agar medium by drawing an 'S' over it using the inoculation loop. Alternatively, you can deposit the spores onto the agar by rubbing the loop over the surface of the medium in a zigzag motion. If possible, try not to open the lid fully but rather open it enough so the loop fits through. You need to work as quickly as possible to avoid the chances of contaminants invading the agar.

Step 3: Seal and Label the Petri Dish

When you have finished scraping the spores onto the agar, you can close the lid and seal it using Parafilm, or masking tape if that is more accessible. Now is also the time to label the petri dish. This will ensure you do not mix up the spores of different species and that you use the spores as soon as possible. You want to include information like the date, strain, and genus name on the label.

Step 4: Watch the Mycelium Grow

You want the spores you have transferred to develop and grow mycelium and, to do so, you need to store them in a dark, sterile environment where they can begin growing. Ideally, you want to keep the inoculated Petri dishes in an incubator or other sterile environment where you can create the ideal conditions and monitor growth. Of course, keep in mind that the conditions will differ from one mushroom species to another. Ensure that the growing space provides adequate ventilation and the proper temperature levels, and you should see the spores begin to germinate within one week. Soon after, rhizomorphic mycelium strands will become visible and you can select those you wish to transfer to a substrate.

When completing this process, it is always best to do it multiple times with the same strain. You can use the spore print more than once to gather spores and transfer them to multiple Petri dishes. Doing this more than once enhances the chances of mycelium growing on the agar and gives you more inoculated plates to work with should one become too contaminated to save. If you use disposable inoculation loops, remember to use a new one for each dish. Metal inoculation loops should be flame sterilized in between every transfer. If you do not wish to work with agar at this stage of the cultivation process, you could opt for using the spore prints to make spore syringes directly.

Making Spore Syringes from Spore Prints

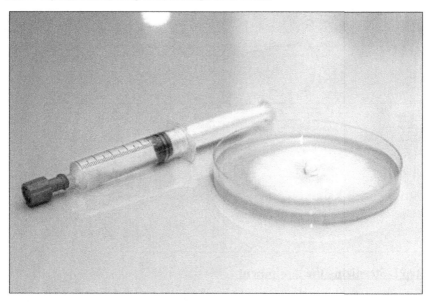

A spore syringe is exactly what it seems: spores are held in a solution that is kept in a syringe until you wish to use it to inoculate the substrate. The spores are mixed with sterile water inside the syringe, ready to be "injected" into the substrate, thereby making it one of the easier germination techniques. But why use a spore syringe? Simple: spore syringes are one of the cleanest methods of inoculation. When using spore syringes, you can add the spores directly to the substrate, which significantly lowers the risk of contamination when done properly. Combine this method with the use of a SAB or flow hood and the risk of contaminating the spawn or substrate should be mitigated quite a bit.

To make spore syringes at home, you need the following:

- A spore print
- A 10 ml or 20 ml sterile syringe
- Sterile water
- A small glass
- A scalpel
- A pair of tweezers
- A pressure cooker
- A burner or gas hob
- A Ziplock or another sealable bag

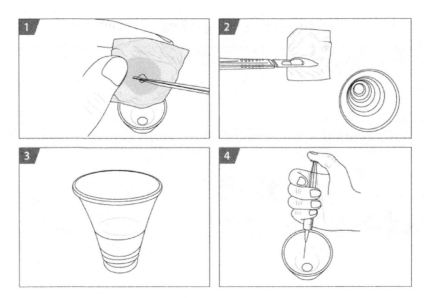

Step 1: Sterilizing the Equipment

You will need to begin the process by sterilizing the small glass and the water in the pressure cooker. You can pour the water into the small glass, place the glass in the pressure cooker, and sterilize it in this manner. The heat of the pressure cooker needs to reach 15 psi; once pressure has been reached, you can lower the temperature and 'cook' the materials for a minimum of 30 minutes. Keeping these materials in the pressure cooker for 30 minutes or more will ensure that they have been properly sterilized. If you plan to reuse syringes, add them to the pressure cooker to be sterilized as well.

Step 2: Allow the Water to Cool

When 30 minutes have passed, turn off the heat entirely and give the water time to cool down to room temperature. You must let the water cool down; mixing the spores with hot water can kill them, which becomes a major problem if you have limited access to them. Your equipment needs to be as sterile as possible, but you will get nowhere if you accidentally kill the spores. It is best to leave the water, and any equipment being sterilized, to cool overnight even if it might feel cool to the touch after a few hours. As you wait for it to cool, be sure to keep the pressure cooker sealed. Opening it before you are ready to use the equipment will lead to it becoming contaminated and you will have to repeat the process again.

Step 3: Making the Syringe

Before working with the water or the spore print, you need to sterilize your tweezers using the burner or another flame source. As the tweezers cool slightly, remove the small glass with water from the pressure cooker. Using the tweezers, take the spore print from storage and hold it over the small glass. With the sterilized scalpel, which you can also clean using a flame, gently scrape spores from one area of the print into the water.

Immediately take the syringe and fill it with spore-filled water. Place the tip of the syringe in the small dish and draw water up into the syringe. To ensure the spores are properly spread throughout the water and that you pick up as many spores as possible, empty the syringe back into the glass and draw water into it again. You can repeat this process a few times. When the syringe has been filled, leave it at room temperature for two or three days to allow the spores to become fully hydrated. After three days, store the spore syringe in an airtight bag, like a Ziplock bag, in the fridge. Spore syringes are viable for at least 12 months, so if you are not able to use them immediately, rest assured that they can be stored.

How to use the Spore Syringe

As alluded to earlier, using a spore syringe is an easy task if it is executed properly. You do not need more than one or two drops, more or less three ml, of spore solution per square liter of the chosen substrate. Simply squirt a few drops into the substrate; the number of drops will depend on the size of the container. Then, you can properly seal the substrate. Within a week, you should see mycelium begin to grow where the solution was dropped. Over the course of a few weeks, these mycelium spots will grow until it has colonized the substrate entirely. As with any other colonization process, keep a close eye on the substrate to ensure that no contaminants grow and that the mycelium spreads throughout the growing medium.

If you do not want to inoculate the spawn directly in this manner, you can use the spore syringe to either form a liquid culture or produce grain spawn on its own from the very start. Both methods will be discussed in detail below.

How to Make Grain Spawn

After creating spore syringes, you will need to use them to make grain spawn so you can begin growing your mushrooms. Keep in mind that you can produce various types of solid spawn and, though the process is the same for all solid spawn, we are taking a more in-depth look at creating grain spawn. Grain spawn is relatively easy to produce at home and, with the step-by-step instructions I provide, you should be able to whip up a batch in no time. Grain spawn is often seen as the traditional or most used way to propagate mushroom cultures. By properly sterilizing the grain and monitoring the moisture content you will quickly see the mycelium expanding, ready to inoculate the substrate.

You can use various grains to make the spawn, like brown rice, wild bird seed, wheat, and rye. Rye is the most used grain in mushroom cultivation because it naturally carries quite a few beneficial nutrients and is known for its water-absorbing attributes. However, grain is only one of the materials you will need to create your own grain spawn. The rest is as follows:

- A five-gallon bucket or another container similar in size
- A stove and large pot
- Jars and polyfill, or polypropylene bags
- A strainer
- A pressure sterilizer

Once you have gathered your materials and chosen a grain, you can begin making your own grain spawn. It is best to choose rye, but you can use another.

Step 1: Rinse and Soak the Grain

The first step in the process is to measure the amount of grain that will be used; keep in mind that grains like rye expand when moistened and often double in size. Your jars need to be about ⅔'s full once fully sterilized. You can use a quart jar to measure one quart of the dry grain for every three quarts of spawn. So, if you only want to make three quarts of spawn, one quart of grain is more than enough. To get your grain ready, you will need to rinse it in cold water roughly five times or until the water runs relatively clear. Move the grains to a bucket and fill it with water; you can also add some gypsum and coffee grounds to this mixture if you wish.

Adding coffee grounds to the water and grains will change the pH and is believed to help increase your yield. The gypsum will aid in preventing the grains from sticking to one another. About a cup of coffee and a tablespoon of gypsum should work perfectly. You can increase this if you plan on making a larger amount of grain spawn. Leave the grains to soak for between 12 and 24 hours; this gives the grains a chance to absorb water. During this time, many contaminants will invade the mixture and begin to sprout but this will make them easier to eliminate during the sterilization process.

Step 2: Cook the Grains

By cooking the grains, they can absorb more water and expand further. The cooking process also softens the grains quite a lot which makes it much easier for the mycelium to digest it. In a large pot, bring the grains to a boil and allow them to simmer for at least 15 minutes. It is possible to cook the grains for too long which will lead to some of the individual grains cracking open and increasing the risk of contamination during the incubation process. So, once the grains have been cooking for 10 minutes, keep a close eye on them. You can remove the pot from the stove a few minutes earlier as long as the grains have softened and swelled.

Step 3: Drain the Grains and Allow them to Dry

Cooking the grains also allows them to dry by releasing steam. Pour the hot grains into a strainer and shake it a few times to allow the steam to escape and evaporate. Once this is done, spread the grains in a thin layer on a tray or towel. Leave the grains to dry for two hours until you don't see any moisture on the outside of the grains. You can pick up a handful of grains to test whether they have dried properly; the grains should be inflated with water on the inside and dry on the outside. The grains should also be loose and not clumped together.

Step 4: Load the Grains

When the grains have dried completely, you can fill your jars to about ⅔ full. You should modify the jar to allow for gas exchange during incubation. When making grain spawn at home, the easiest way to do this is by drilling a quarter-inch hole through the lid and pulling some synthetic pillow stuffing through the drilled hole. This will keep contaminants away from the spawn while giving the mycelium space to breathe. Creating a hole in the lid also makes inoculation with a spore syringe easier because you can inject it through the stuffing. Finally, cover the lids with tinfoil to prevent the water from the pressure cooker from getting into the jar and changing the moisture levels of the grain.

Step 5: Sterilize the Grains

For this step, you can use either a pressure cooker, an autoclave, or any equipment that allows for steam sterilization. To be adequately sterilized, you will need to keep the grains in the pressure cooker at 15 psi for 90 minutes. The 90-minute period starts once the pressure has reached 15 psi and not a moment before that. When 90 minutes have passed, turn off the pressure cooker and leave the grain jars to cool for a few hours. Move the jars to a clean environment, where you plan to grow your mushrooms, and inspect the grains. Very few of the individual grains should be broken, and none should be clumped together. Once your inspection is complete, you now have grain that is ready to be inoculated with mushroom spawn.

How to Inoculate Grain Spawn

Grain jars that have been sterilized and cooled down can be inoculated immediately with either agar or a spore syringe. However, the sterilized grains are incredibly susceptible to contamination so you cannot work with them if you cannot use an aseptic technique or work in an aseptic environment. Ideally, you want to use a SAB or flow hood to inoculate the grains. Be sure to clean and disinfect the workspace and the tools you will use before getting started. Using an aseptic technique also involves ensuring your hands are clean and wearing protective gear like gloves, a face mask, etc.

When inoculating the grains with a spore syringe, you must sterilize the needle before injecting the spores into the grains. Carefully remove the layer of tin foil from the lid and inject a few drops of the liquid into the jar via the hole you drilled in the lid. If you are inoculating more than one jar, be sure to sterilize the needle between every jar. When inoculating with agar, cut a small piece of agar from a colonized plate with a sterile scalpel. As quickly as you can, open the lid and place the piece of agar in the jar. Reseal the jar as soon as you are done to avoid contamination. You now have grain spawn which, when the mycelium has spread, can be used to inoculate a substrate and grow mushrooms. If neither of these is the method you wish to use, you could always opt for making and using liquid culture, which is an additional step to making spore syringes and producing solid spawn like grain spawn.

Liquid Culture

Though you certainly can simply inject the spore solution in the syringe directly into the grains, there is an extra step you can take to turn the spore syringe into liquid culture and inoculate the grains in that way. Liquid culture, unlike spore syringes, is living mushroom mycelium in slightly nutritious water so the spore syringes contain spores and liquid culture contains mycelium. The water consists of about 500 ml of non-chlorinated, filtered water mixed with 10 grams of some type of fermentable sugar. This is typically the ratio, but you can adjust it to suit your needs. Many cultivators prefer using liquid cultures because you do not need to create a sterile environment before inoculating the grains. The risk of liquid culture being contaminated and thereby contaminating the grains is very low which means the chances of failure are also significantly lower.

As mentioned, spore syringes are filled with a spore solution while liquid culture is made from nutritious water and mycelium. For spores to become mycelium, they must first have the opportunity to germinate. So, when inoculating the grains using a spore syringe, the spores need to germinate before they can grow mycelium. Liquid culture inoculates the grains with mycelium immediately and begins growing more immediately. Therefore, using liquid culture is an excellent way to save time while growing mushrooms.

Making Liquid Culture

As with agar plates and spore syringes, you can make liquid culture at home. To do so, you will need the following:

- 1 liter of water
- 40 grams of light malt extract
- 1 gram brewer's yeast
- A magnetic stirrer
- Four 16-ounce jars with modified lids
- A pressure cooker
- Tin foil

The jars you will be using need to be modified to house liquid culture as fresh air exchange is vital to healthy development. However, mycelium releases quite a bit of carbon dioxide as it grows, lowering oxygen levels in an unmodified jar. To combat this and introduce more oxygen into the jars, you will need to make some changes to the lids. You can modify the jar lids by adding a filter that will aid in fresh air exchange and creating an injection port allowing you to inject liquid and extract material without risking contamination.

Once the lids have been modified, you can begin making liquid culture by following the steps below.

Step 1: Measuring and Mixing a Liquid Culture Broth

Carefully measure out the brewer's yeast and the light malt; you need to use the exact measurements when making the mixture to ensure the liquid culture will remain healthy. Mix the malt extract and the brewer's yeast with water and fill the mason jars halfway with the liquid culture broth. Add a magnetic stir rod into each jar after filling them. This will help you break up any clumps of mycelium that might form later. Screw the modified lids onto the jars and cover each one with a piece of tin foil.

Step 2: Sterilize the Liquid Culture Broth

Sterilize the broth at 15 psi for 20 minutes using equipment like an autoclave or pressure canner. Much like sterilizing grain for grain spawn, wait to begin the timer until the pressure has reached 15 psi. Once 20 minutes have passed, leave the pressure canner or cooker to cool completely before opening it and removing the jars.

Step 3: Inoculating the Liquid Culture Broth

Once the jars have cooled down, you can inoculate the broth with live mycelium culture. When inoculating the broth, it is incredibly important to use aseptic techniques; liquid cultures lower the risk of contamination considerably but are not immune to it. Be sure to clean all tools used with rubbing alcohol and flame sterilize the needles used with the syringe especially if you use the same syringe multiple times. You can add your mycelium sample using a syringe and injecting it via the injection port. Alternatively, you can add mycelium that has been grown on agar by using a flow hood or SAB and carefully removing the lid and inserting the sample.

Step 4: Agitate the Mixture

Now that the sample has been added, store your jar in an area with a temperature between 64°F and 68°F. Give the mixture a few days to settle after which you must stir it daily to keep the mycelium from becoming too cloudy or clumping together. You can either stir it by hand or use a magnetic stirrer which can easily be found online or, if you prefer, you can find a guide to make your own. When you agitate the mixture, keep the liquid as far away from the lid as possible or you might draw contaminants to it.

Step 5: Give the Mycelium Time to Grow

Stirring the mixture daily, you should see a significant amount of mycelium grow within 14 - 21 days. When the mycelium has begun growing in large amounts, you can use it to inoculate grain spawn or create agar plates and more liquid cultures. It is best to test the liquid culture for contaminants before using it to inoculate grain. You can do this by introducing a few drops to an agar plate to ensure there are no contaminants in the mixture. Once you have verified that the liquid culture is contaminant free, you can use it to inoculate grains and create grain spawn. Like spore syringes, you can add a few drops to the grains and wait for the mycelium to grow.

You now have all the tools you need to create your own spawn using mushroom spore prints. In the next section, we will be looking at a second method that you can use which involves essentially cloning a mushroom. As with this first method, I will walk you through the entire process step-by-step, so let's get right into it.

Method 2: Producing Spawn Through Cloning Mushrooms or Using Stem Butts

If you think you might not like making your own spawn from spores prints, you could opt to use this second method which involves making spawn from stem butts, or a process that some cultivators refer to as cloning mushrooms. Though it may seem complicated, mushroom cloning is relatively easy and can be done at home without purchasing expensive equipment. In addition to the relatively simple nature of the process, it can also be done with or without using agar. In this section, I will guide you through both methods and you can decide for yourself which one you prefer to use. Before tackling the step-by-step process, let us first learn some of the basic knowledge needed to clone mushrooms.

What is Mushroom Cloning?

Mushroom cloning essentially entails using a living piece of the fruiting body to create an identical copy of the chosen mushroom. Cultivators use the term "cloning" because you are making a genetically identical copy of the mushroom organism. The great thing about this method is that it can be done with fresh mushrooms; so as long as the mushrooms are freshly harvested, you can use them to create your own spawn. Mushrooms are made up of tightly packed mycelium which is still alive and fit to reproduce even after it has been harvested. You need only take a piece of the mushroom's living tissue, and place it in a growing medium full of nutrients, and the mycelium will begin to grow and spread through the medium. This mycelium can then be used again to grow more mushrooms. The cycle is endless!

At this point, you may be asking yourself what the benefits of cloning mushrooms are, and quite a few may persuade you to use this method to produce your own spawn. Below are only a few of the advantages to consider when deciding whether or not to use this method:

- Mushroom cloning allows you to create a copy of the perfect mushroom. You can choose a healthy mushroom with a large yield, that grows quickly, has a lovely color, and so on.

- You can clone foraged, store-bought, or freshly harvested mushrooms that you have grown yourself, so there is no need to go hunting for specific mushrooms because you can clone what is readily available.

- This process is easier and quicker than growing mushrooms from spores; it is often difficult to find viable spores and the growth period with cloning is not as long.

Using Agar to Clone Mushrooms

By using agar to clone your mushrooms, you lower the risk of contaminants invading the mushrooms' growing space. However, remember that this method can seem a little bit daunting for beginners even if it is a lot of fun.

You will need the following supplies:

- A large, young mushroom
- Agar plates
- A clean environment like a SAB or flow hood
- An alcohol-soaked cloth
- A scalpel
- A steady flame like an alcohol burner
- Protective gear - gloves, face mask, hair net
- Parafilm
- A marker

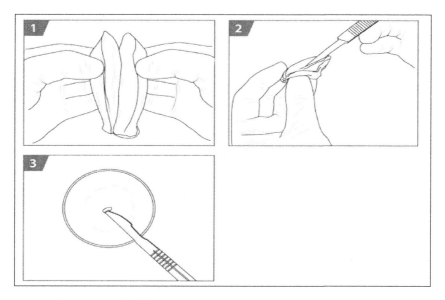

Step 1: Preparing the Workspace

As with the other methods, and when growing mushrooms in general, it is important that you keep the workspace clean. Regularly clean your hands and the work surface and use protective gear when possible. It is also ideal to perform these tasks in a sterile environment like a SAB or laminar flow hood.

Step 2: Preparing the Mushroom

Before cloning the mushroom, you need to clean it gently using a cloth or paper towel soaked in alcohol. It is important to methodically clean the outside of the fruiting body as this is typically the part that carries contaminants that may move to the agar plate. After cleaning the mushroom, you must tear it open in front of the laminar flow hood while keeping it downstream of the agar plate. Tearing instead of cutting open the mushroom will help prevent contamination. Torn mushrooms are naturally sterile and hold clean, fertile mycelium cells. When you cut mushrooms, the knife's edge will push those contaminants on the outside of the fruiting body inwards its center.

Step 3: Sterilizing the Scalpel

You will use the scalpel to remove a tissue sample from the fruiting body, so it needs to be as clean as possible. To achieve this, you will need heat to sterilize the scalpel. It needs to be sterilized between each transfer therefore it is best to keep a constant, steady flame on your work surface; you could use either an alcohol burner or an alcohol lamp. Allow the scalpel to cool completely before use or you risk destroying the mushroom tissue. You can cool the scalpel by dipping the blade into agar near the edge of the dish - you should hear it sizzle as it cools. When using this method, work as quickly as possible and ensure the lid is replaced properly. Alternatively, you can heat the scalpel before tearing the mushroom and let it cool in the air of the flow hood as you prepare the fruiting body.

Step 4: Removing and Transferring the Tissue

Because the entire mushroom is made up of dense mycelium, the tissue used for cloning can be taken from any part of the fruiting body. However, tissue taken from specific areas does produce better results. When harvesting reproductive cells, it is best to remove tissue from one of these parts:

- The middle part of the stem directly below the cap.
- The middle, fleshy part of the stem butt.
- The underside of the cap, relatively close to the mushroom gills.

However, when removing tissue for cloning, avoid using the gills. They are very tricky to clean and contain spores that can germinate in the agar thereby changing the mushroom strain.

Scrape the scalpel across the flesh of the chosen area a few times to remove some tissue. Alternatively, you can cut a small piece of tissue away, no bigger than 0.12-inch x 1.02-inch. Use the tip of the scalpel to move the tissue to the agar plate, keeping it upstream of the plate. Then remove the lid and place the piece of tissue on the agar. Then close the dish immediately. Work quickly and carefully because the plate needs to be open for the shortest time possible. Though optional, it is best to repeat this process one or two more times, sterilizing the scalpel between each removal and transfer. Once done, you should have at least three pieces of tissue on the agar plate. Having more than one piece will improve your chances of success.

Step 5: Sealing, Incubating and Cleaning the Agar Plate

You can now use the parafilm to seal the inoculated plates and label them with the inoculation date and species name using the marker. Parafilm creates a tight seal on the agar plates while allowing them to breathe. Move the sealed plates to a spot away from any direct sunlight. That will maintain room temperature to allow it to inoculate. It can take up to three days for the mycelium to begin growing from the tissue towards the edges of the plate. The mushroom culture will be clean on your first try if you are lucky. However, there will often be spots of green or black fungus growing on the agar, indicating contamination. Should this happen, you can once again use a sterilized scalpel to remove some of the uncontaminated mycelium and transfer it to a new, clean agar plate. This process may have to be repeated a few times before the mushroom culture is entirely clean.

Step 6: Storing the Mushroom Culture

You will need to use or store the mushroom culture before the mycelium spreads to the edges of the agar plate. Waiting too long could lead to the mycelium growing through the parafilm and becoming contaminated. There are a few types of mushroom cultures that can be stored in the fridge and will remain viable for about a year, but others (like pink oysters) will not survive the cold conditions. If you are planning to use this method to grow mushrooms, it is always best to do additional research on how to store the specific species you will be cultivating.

How to Clone Mushrooms Without Using Agar

You can use several methods to clone mushrooms without using agar, each related to a different substrate, but using the same process. It is important to note that methods not utilizing agar are at higher risk of contamination. For beginner cultivators, some of these techniques can be quite fun, so let's dive into a few ways you can clone mushrooms without using agar.

Method 1: Cloning Directly into Sterilized Grains

The process of cloning mushrooms using grains is quite similar to cloning mushrooms using agar. The only major difference is that instead of using agar plates, you use directly sterilized jars of grain spawn. One of the significant disadvantages of this method that you need to take note of, involves contamination. It is more challenging to see and identify other fungi or mold when using jars of grain spawn than you would on a 2D surface like agar plates. As I mentioned when describing the process of making grain spawn, you can use just about any type of grain to create spawn and to clone your mushrooms, but rye remains the best and easiest source to use as it has all of the nutrients the mushrooms will need and it holds water well.

Method 2: Cloning Using Sterilized Cardboard

You can also clone your mushrooms on sterilized cardboard if you do not want to use agar or grain. With this method, keep in mind that the risk of contamination is higher than average. In addition, this type of cultivation only works on mushrooms that are not as picky about their growing medium, like oyster mushrooms. This method is much like that of cloning using agar with a few simple variations. You will be pushing the cut or scraped tissue into the ribs of the sterilized cardboard instead of on agar. When the tissue has been placed, you will need to move the inoculated cardboard into a sterilized jar to allow the mycelium and mushroom to grow.

With this final method discussed, you can now create your own mushroom spawn at home. Some of these techniques will take time to refine and get the hang of, but with practice you can continuously make your own mushrooms at home. In the final chapter, we will go over ten DIY mushroom-growing projects, most of which can be done by growing your own spawn. Whether you prefer buying kits or using premade spawn, I recommend that you try to make your own spawn at least once in your cultivating journey. It allows you to learn much more about mushrooms and how they grow, and it can be a lot of fun. Now, without further ado, let's jump into the ten mushroom-growing projects.

CHAPTER 13

Ten Mushroom Projects to do at Home

Over the course of this book, I have taught you all of the theoretical aspects of mushroom cultivation you should be familiar with to be successful. In this final chapter, we put this theory into practice by looking at ten different ways you can grow mushrooms at home. All the mushroom cultivation processes mentioned in this chapter have to do with mushrooms discussed earlier in this book. These are all beginner-friendly, and I offer you a step-by-step guide on completing each one successfully. After this chapter, you will be able to grow mushrooms indoors and outdoors, prepare the substrate, inoculate the substrate, and so on. Let's not waste any more time and jump straight into the first project.

Indoor Cultivation Projects

Growing Mushrooms in Straw Bags

Project 1: Growing Pink Oyster Mushrooms on Straw

The process of cultivating pink oyster mushrooms is much the same as cultivating other oyster mushrooms. However, there are some key differences in the procedure, so we must go over the growing process in detail.

To begin growing pink oyster mushrooms, you will need the following materials:

- Pink oyster mushroom spawn. Grain spawn is recommended over sawdust spawn, as it will have a higher yield.
- Straw to use as a substrate. Straw is the best substrate for pink oyster mushrooms and allows quick colonization. It is recommended that the straw chips be no longer than 1-3". A good ratio is about 3 pounds of spawn to 20 pounds of straw.
- A large container for mixing (a large plastic box, a barrel, a bucket, or what you have available)
- Growing bags (polypropylene bags) or similar containers

Growing pink oysters on straw requires you to take the following steps:

1. Substrate Preparation

- Prepare the substrate by chopping it to the correct size.

2. Pasteurization

- Pasteurize the straw using one of the two methods discussed earlier: a warm water bath or a cold water lime bath.
- If you opt for the cold water lime bath, consider soaking the straw in hot water (160-170°F) for 1-2 hours.
- In the case of cold water lime bath, wash the straw for 12-18 hours.

3. Inoculation

- Use pink oyster mushroom spawn to inoculate the straw substrate by mixing it in a large container.
- Before mixing the straw and the spawn, it is important that you check that the straw has the proper moisture content. Your moisture content should be in the range of 55%-75%. You can do a simple test to ensure the correct moisture content. Squeeze the straw in your hand, and a couple of drops of water should come out. If more drops leak out, you will need to dry your straw more. If you cannot get any drops, you will need to add more water to the straw.

- Move the mixture to a proper growing container like a plastic bag. If you are not using a filter, cut a few holes in the bag using the technique mentioned in the previous section

4. Incubation

- Place the bag in a sterile environment and maintain ideal incubation conditions. To avoid early pinning, you should use a warm room (about 70°F) with no direct light. Indirect light is advised.
- Check on the bag frequently and watch as the white mycelium spreads and colonizes the substrate.

5. Fruiting

- Once the bag has been completely colonized, fruiting can begin.
- Enhance the light levels, mist the bags a few times a day, and maintain a temperature between 50°F and 86°F. You should see pins begin to form in five to seven days. The mushroom will typically start to fruit within 1-2 weeks and will be ready to harvest within 2-4 weeks.

6. Harvesting

- Watch your pink oyster mushrooms double in size daily. You can harvest the fruiting bodies when the caps begin to flatten out by twisting the base and pulling them off.

Project 2: Growing Shiitake Mushrooms on Straw

Growing shiitake mushrooms at home can be manageable and easy, and you do not need a lot of expensive equipment to do it. Like oyster mushrooms, some strains of shiitake can grow on a straw-based substrate. Using straw, easily attainable, as a substrate, you can cultivate shiitake mushrooms indoors. In this section, we'll go over the process of growing shiitake mushrooms on straw.

To grow your shiitake mushrooms, you will need the following materials:

- Nutrient-rich straw to use as substrate
- Shiitake mushroom spawn
- Polypropylene bags or other appropriate growing containers
- A large container in which to mix the substrate and spawn

When you have gathered all of your materials, you can implement the following steps:

1. Substrate Preparation & Pasteurization

- Before introducing the spawn to the straw substrate, you must first properly prepare the substrate. You will need to pasteurize the substrate using either a cold-water lime bath or heated water. When using the hot water technique, ensure the temperature is between 149°F and 176°F, and leave it in the bath for two hours. Soak it for at least 12-18 hours if using the cold-water lime bath method. For more details, you can read the same section of the first project, where I have given more information on the pasteurization of straw.

2. Inoculation

- When the substrate has been prepared, you can inoculate it using the shiitake spawn. This is done by mixing the two in a large container until you are sure the spawn has been evenly distributed.

- After the substrate has been inoculated, you can transfer the mixture to the grow bag and close the top by twisting and securing it with a rubber band.

3. Incubation

- Like oyster varieties, Shiitake mushrooms can take a bit longer to incubate than other mushrooms. Storing the bags in a dark place at room temperature will help the mycelium colonize the substrate. Unlike other species, the mycelium of shiitake mushrooms must be left to turn brown before they begin to fruit. Once they have turned white, the browning can take about two weeks. The incubation process can also last several months.

4. Fruiting

- When the mycelium has spread completely, open the growing bags and place the spawn block in a humid area with a lot of fresh air exchange. The shiitake grows reasonably fast at this stage, and the first flush should appear in one week.

- Mist the block a few times every day to keep it moist because shiitake mushrooms grow well when given water regularly.

5. Harvesting

- Let your shiitake mushrooms grow to a decent size before harvesting them. With these mushrooms, it is best to use a sharp knife to cut them at the base instead of twisting them.

- Please do not throw away your spawn block, as it should be able to produce from three to five flushes before the mycelium is completely spent.

Project 3: Growing Oyster Mushrooms in Coco Coir and Vermiculite Bags

Oyster mushrooms can grow on a variety of different substrates, and coco coir and vermiculite are no exceptions. In this section, we'll be taking a look at the process of growing oyster mushrooms using this substrate.

You will need to gather the following materials:

- Coco coir mixed with vermiculite substrate. The ratio between Coco coir and vermiculate should be 1:1. A block of coco coir usually weighs 1.43 pounds (650 grams). You can pair the block with 8 cups of dry vermiculite.
- Powdered gypsum for additional minerals (optional). When adding gypsum, the substrate is also known as **CVG** (**C**oir **V**ermiculite and **G**ypsum). The gypsum helps to stabilize the pH and enables higher yields by providing additional minerals. One cup of gypsum should be enough. Another option is to add coffee grounds to provide extra nitrogen.
- Oyster mushroom spawn of your choice. I recommend using grain spawn.
- A container to mix and prepare the substrate for the inoculation.
- Polypropylene bags or a Fruiting Chamber for the incubation and fruiting.

The steps to grow oyster mushrooms on this type of substrate are as follows:

1. Substrate Preparation

- Prepare the substrate using the mixing method detailed in Chapter 8 of this book, i.e. breaking down the coco coir block with boiling water in a lidded container, adding the vermiculite and mixing it. Close the lid and let it cool to room temperature. Based on the quantities of coco coir and vermiculite previously specified, you will need 16 cups of hot water at the temperature of 165°F.
- When the substrate has cooled completely (it should take approximately 6 to 8 hours), you can mix the ingredients with a spoon or with your hands.
- To ensure that substrate is at the proper humidity level, you can use the "squeeze test" described in the previous projects.

2. Inoculation

- Mix the spawn into the container you used for the substrate preparation, ensuring it has been distributed evenly. The spawn rate needs to be at 20% of the spawn rate of the wet substrate. You must ensure that the substrate has cooled down, or the heat will kill the mycelium.
- Transfer the mixed materials to the grow bags or chosen containers for incubation. For this type of mix, it is common to use a Monotub as a fruiting chamber.

3. Incubation

- Place the filled bags in a dark, warm area with temperatures between 65°F and 77°F and leave the bags to allow the mycelium to spread. If you find it difficult to replicate such conditions, using a fruiting chamber such as a Martha Grow Tent, Shotgun Fruiting Chamber, or a Monotub can be a good idea.

- Oyster mushroom mycelium should spread quickly and entirely when the substrate surface is covered in white. It isn't easy to estimate the time required as it depends on the spawn rate as well as on the composition of the substrate, whether you have included gypsum, coffee ground, etc...

4. Fruiting

- When the mycelium has spread, pins will begin to form near the holes of the grow bag/container, and, as the mushrooms double in size, the fruiting bodies will push through the holes as they seek a change in light, temperatures, humidity, and airflow.

5. Harvesting

- Once the mushroom caps begin to flatten out, you can harvest them by twisting the mushrooms at the base and gently pulling them from the substrate.

Growing Mushrooms on Supplemented Hardwood Sawdust

Project 4: Growing Lion's Mane Mushrooms in Sawdust Bags

Though lion's mane, like many other mushrooms, can be grown on a variety of substrates, it produces the best results on supplemented hardwood sawdust. The most common supplement is wheat or oat bran, usually at 10% to 20%. Growing these mushrooms in bags is one of the most commonly used methods and can be done at home without the need for specialized equipment.

I recommend to use grains, ideally Rye grains, as spawn. Ensure to shake the grains often to ensure full colonization of the spawn.

You will need the following supplies:

- Water
- Growing bags
- Lion's mane mushroom spawn
- Wheat or oat bran
- Hardwood pellets
- A scale
- A bucket
- A measuring cup

In order to grow lion's mane at home, you will need to do the following:

1. Substrate Preparation & Sterilization

- Take the time to prepare the substrate properly; you want it to be as nutrient-rich and hydrated as possible to allow for mycelium growth.

- To produce a five-pound block of supplemented hardwood substrate, you will need to mix five cups of hardwood pellets, six cups of water, and one-and-a-quarter cups of your chosen type of bran.

- Let the pellets soak in a bucket with water for 30 minutes to allow them to break apart and form sawdust. Add the bran and mix it until everything is well incorporated.

- Squeeze the substrate to test that the moisture content is adequate; only a few drops of water should escape.

- Transfer the mixture to a grow bag, remove as much air as possible and fold the bag closed.

- Sterilize the substrate in a pressure canner or cooker at 15 psi for two and a half hours.

- Leave the substrate to cool for eight hours before inoculation

2. Inoculation

- Add the lion's mane spawn to the cooled-down substrate at a 5% spawn rate per bag of the wet substrate. Mix to distribute the spawn evenly, twist the top of the bag closed, and tie it with a rubber band

3. Incubation

- Leave the bags to incubate in a dark area with temperatures between 68°F and 75°F. It should take three weeks for the mycelium to colonize the substrate fully. The mycelium of Lion's mane is not as dense as that of other mushrooms like Oysters, so don't be surprised if the bag doesn't seem to be completely colonized

4. Fruiting

- When the substrate has been fully incubated, you can cut holes in the bag to expose the colonized substrate to fresh air and move the bags to a shady, humid area. Mist the substrate several times a day to ensure that it remains moist. Pinheads should form within three days and grow into mature mushrooms that can be harvested within two weeks. Even in this case, using one of the fruiting chambers described in this book can help to control all the fruiting variables. The ideal fruiting temperature for Lion's Mane is between 60°F and 70°F and you should keep humidity at 90%

5. Harvesting

- Harvest the mushrooms before they change color by cutting the body off at the base close to the substrate with a sharp knife. Work gently, as the mushrooms last longer when not damaged.

Project 5: Growing Reishi Mushrooms in Sawdust Bags

Reishi mushrooms, often used for medicinal benefits, can also be grown indoors in supplemented hardwood sawdust bags. The process of growing these mushrooms does not differ very much from the lion's mane cultivation process described above. As with lion's mane mushrooms, growing reishi at home is quite simple and beginner friendly.

When you're ready to grow these, gather the following supplies:

- Reishi mushroom spawn. I recommend using grain spawn as it is easier to mix with the substrate. Alternatively, you can use sawdust spawn.
- Hardwood sawdust substrate with a supplement of oat or wheat bran. You can use the recipe from the previous project
- A bucket or large container for mixing
- Large polypropylene grow bags with filter patches that can withstand the substrate sterilization process

After you have gathered the supplies, use the following steps to grow your reishi mushrooms:

1. Substrate Preparation

- Using the same process described in the previous project, prepare the hardwood substrate for inoculation. To prepare five lb. of the substrate, you need five cups of hardwood pellets, one-and-a-quarter-cup of oat or wheat bran, and six cups of water.

2. Inoculation

- In a bucket or container, mix the reishi spawn with the substrate. You will want to add the spawn at roughly a 5% spawn rate to the wet hardwood sawdust substrate. Mix the spawn and substrate until the spawn has been thoroughly distributed through the substrate.

- When the spawn and substrate have been mixed, transfer the mixture to a growing bag and close the top with a rubber band.

3. Incubation

- Move the bag to a dark area where it can incubate at room temperature. The reishi mycelium will begin to grow through and colonize the substrate. The substrate should be entirely colonized between 10 and 14 days.

4. Fruiting

- To encourage fruiting, ensure the temperature is between 75°F and 85°F, or the mushrooms might take longer to begin pinning. Reishi mushrooms can take 30 to 45 days to be ready for harvesting.

- Ensure a humidity level in the range of 85% to 90%.

5. Harvesting

- When ready to harvest, use a sharp knife to cut the mushrooms from the substrate.

Growing Mushrooms on Cardboard

Project 6: Growing Oyster Mushrooms on Cardboard

You will find that oyster mushrooms are not very picky when it comes to the type of substrate they grow on. For this reason, you can use some of the cardboard you have lying around at home to grow oyster mushrooms. Not only is this a great way to grow mushrooms indoors, but you can also recycle some cardboard instead of throwing it away.

Before beginning the growing process, you will need to create cardboard spawn. The process is quite straightforward and should pose no problems for first-time cultivators. To produce this spawn, you will need the following supplies:

- Fresh oyster mushroom stems
- Several large cardboard pieces
- A large bucket
- Filtered water
- A plastic container

Once the supplies have been gathered, the process is simple. You will need to tear the cardboard into smaller pieces and pasteurize it using boiling water. Give the cardboard a few hours to cool down before layering it in a container along with the oyster mushroom stem butts. Move the container to a cool, dark place and wait roughly three weeks for the mycelium to completely colonize the cardboard.

When you have created this mushroom spawn, you can begin growing your oyster mushrooms.

To have a plentiful and healthy yield, you will need to transfer the mushrooms into grow bags or buckets with more cardboard that will be your substrate. In order to do so, take the following steps

1. Substrate Preparation

- Carefully examine the spawn to ensure that no contaminations have invaded the material. If the spawn has been contaminated, it is best to throw it away and start from scratch. Spawn that is white and fluffy is ready for use.

2. Pasteurization

- Break any remaining or new clean cardboard into smaller pieces and pasteurize it before adding it to the grow bags. I recommend using a bucket for doing the pasteurization process. Ideally, you want the cardboard pieces to be between one and four inches.

3. Inoculation

- Squeeze the excess water out of the cooled cardboard and begin layering it in the grow bags along with the mushroom spawn. The optimal spawn rate when growing oyster mushrooms is roughly 90% cardboard and 10% oyster mushroom spawn.
- Secure the top of the bag with a rubber band so it will remain closed for the growth cycle.

4. Incubation

- Move the grow bag to a dark place where they can incubate for the next two or three weeks.

5. Fruiting

- When the mycelium has spread fully, and the bag is covered in white, the mushrooms are ready to fruit. Cut a few holes in the grow bag through which the mushrooms can grow.
- Mist the mycelium a few times a day to help the mushrooms fruit correctly.
- Pins should form within a few days after opening the bag, and mature mushrooms should appear within seven days.

6. Harvesting

- Harvest the oyster mushrooms by twisting them at the base and pulling them gently from the substrate.

Growing Mushrooms in Bottles and Jars

Project 7: Growing Cordyceps in Jars

Cordyceps are an excellent mushroom to grow in glass bottles or jars, especially if you do not have a lot of indoor cultivation space. Growing cordyceps in jars or bottles can seem like a daunting task when looking at the supplies needed, but it is quite simple.

These are the supplies you will need:

- Brown rice or rye wheat substrate
- Cordyceps liquid culture
- Nutrient broth
- Nutritional yeast
- Filtered water
- Pureed vegetables
- Starch

- Sugar
- Trace minerals
- Jars with wide mouths
- A face mask
- Gloves
- Polyfill
- Isopropyl alcohol

Substrate Preparation

Before you can inoculate the growing substrate, you will first need to create the media and a nutrient broth. The recipe for the broth is as follows:

- 4-and-a-half-liters of water
- 2 tablespoons of sugar
- 2 tablespoons of trace mineral powder
- 2 tablespoons of rice per jar
- ½ cup of starch
- ¼ cup of nutritional yeast
- 5 scoops of pureed vegetables

With this recipe, you can produce the media using the following steps:

1. Drill a small hole in the lid of each jar.
2. Use isopropyl alcohol to sterilize the inside and the outside of the jar.
3. Use a small amount of polyfill to stuff the hole. This will act as a filter.
4. Mix all of the ingredients together, except the rice. Everything should be dissolved.
5. Add the rice to the jars.
6. Add ¼ cup of liquid to each jar.
7. Screw the lid on tightly and use a pressure cooker (or similar equipment) to sterilize the jars at 240°F for three hours.
8. Let the jars cool down overnight before inoculating them with spawn.

Once you have prepared the jars, complete the following steps to successfully grow cordyceps:

1. Using the liquid culture, inject 10 ml of the cordyceps spawn into the jars through the polyfill filter. Shift the needle around a bit to ensure the culture is spread evenly.

2. Seal the jars and move them to a dark environment with temperatures between 53°F and 75°F. It can take between 10 and 20 days for the mycelium to fully colonize the substrate.

3. When the substrate has been fully colonized, you can introduce the jars to 16 hours of indirect light a day to aid in fruiting. The temperature should remain the same, any higher and you risk killing the fruiting body. The jars should remain closed while the mushrooms pin and mature; this process can take between four and six weeks.

4. Cordyceps grow on top of the substrate, usually reaching close to the inside of the lid. As soon as the fruiting body stops growing, and before it touches the lid, you can harvest your mushrooms by twisting them off at the base.

With the process of growing cordyceps in jars or bottles, our indoor cultivation projects come to an end. The last few projects revolve around growing mushrooms outdoors and are just as beginner friendly as the indoor projects.

Outdoor Cultivation Projects

Growing Mushrooms on Logs

Project 8: Growing King Oyster Mushrooms on Logs

Oyster Mushrooms on Log/Credit: www.northspore.com

King oysters are a wonderful oyster variant to grow outside on logs. Due to the size of its fruiting body, cultivators often opt for growing these mushrooms outside instead of inside where they may not have enough space to properly flourish. Let's dive into the process of growing king oyster mushrooms on logs.

You will need the following materials:

- Pre-cut fresh white birch logs (oak, maple and elm work just as well)
- King oyster mushroom spawn plugs
- A drill
- A 5/16th drill bit
- Beeswax
- A hammer

Once all the supplies have been gathered, you can use the following steps to grow your king oyster mushrooms on logs

1. Substrate preparation

- Once the logs have been cut, whether you cut them yourself or buy pre-cut logs, let them rest for two weeks before beginning the process. Waiting longer than two weeks can lead to contamination. Ideally, the logs should be three to eight inches in diameter and 36 to 40 inches in length.

2. Inoculation

- The best period to inoculate your log is in May when the risk of frost is very low.

- Determine how many spawn plugs you will need. For a log that is 40 inches long, 30 plugs should be enough. If you want to be more specific, you can use the formula: length of the log x diameter of the log / 60 = number of holes.

- When you have decided on a number of king oyster spawn plugs, drill the holes into the log. First, drill a row of holes six inches apart down the length of the log. Each hole should be about 1 inch deep. Then, once the first row is done, begin on the second but stagger the holes; they should be 2.5 inches from the first row and form a checkerboard pattern.

- Using a hammer, gently insert the plug spawn dowels into the holes. Ensure the plugs sit deep enough to flush with the log's wood.

- Use beeswax to seal the holes to ensure the mycelium is safe from contamination. Heat the wax until it is pourable, and use a small brush to cover the plugs with a light coating to seal them. This keeps the moisture in for a while and keeps contaminants out. You can heat the wax with a pot on the stovetop.

3. Incubation

- Store your logs in a shady area with good humidity and airflow.

- Water the logs twice a week for 10 minutes to keep their moisture levels up.

- It can take six to nine months for the mycelium to colonize the entire log.

4. Fruiting

- In addition, it can take up to three years before your mushrooms begin to pin and mature. To speed up the process, you can shock your logs by soaking them in cold water for 24 hours. You can use a pond, an inflatable swimming pool, a container for rainwater harvesting, etc...

- Before shocking your logs with cold water, you should wait six to nine months to allow the mycelium to grow into the logs.

5. Harvesting

- Mushrooms grown on logs will fruit once or twice a year, depending on the environment. You can harvest your king oyster mushrooms by using a sharp knife to cut them off near the base.

- Fully grown mushrooms can grow even after a few days. Ensure that you harvest them on time. If you wait too long, mushrooms will be too woody to be eaten or might attract insects.

Project 9: Growing Shiitake Mushrooms on Logs

The process of growing shiitake mushrooms on logs is not that much different than the process of growing king oyster mushrooms on logs as described above. With a few differences in time, temperature and so on, getting these mushrooms to grow on logs requires following many of the same steps. So, let's get into the process.

You will need the following supplies:

- A fresh cut log, usually oak works best for shiitake mushrooms
- Shiitake plug spawn
- A drill
- A 5/16th drill bit
- A hammer
- Beeswax

When you have gathered your supplies, use the steps below to begin growing your shiitake mushrooms:

1. Cut the logs, or buy pre-cut logs, using the same measurements as for king oyster mushrooms.

2. Drill holes in the logs. The measurements should be the same as those mentioned in the previous project.

3. Use the hammer to lightly knock the plug spawn dowels into the holes. Seal the plugs with a light layer of melted beeswax.

4. Transfer the logs to a shady location and leave them to incubate for between six and twelve months. If you have access to them, you can use a few bricks to elevate the logs and prevent contamination.

5. Water the logs for 10 minutes, once a week.

6. Shiitake mushrooms can begin fruiting on logs naturally between six and twelve months. If you want them to fruit sooner, you can shock the shiitake logs by soaking them in cold water for 24 hours. The pins should begin growing after two weeks.

7. You can harvest shiitake mushrooms by using a sharp knife to cut them off at the base of the stem. Shiitake mushrooms are usually read to be harvested in two to seven days from when they begin to grow. You should harvest them while their cap is still closed and the diameter of their cap is not larger than 5cm.

Growing Mushrooms on Compost

Project 10: Growing White Button Mushrooms on Compost

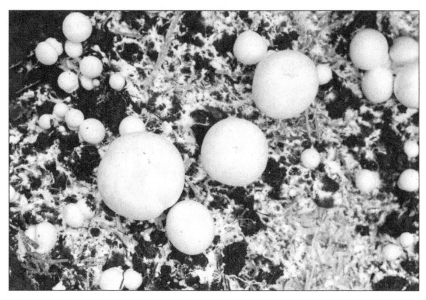

Our final DIY project involves growing white button mushrooms on compost. White button mushrooms grow very well on a compost mixture which you can make at home. The good thing about white button mushrooms is that they can be grown outside in a shady spot, and you do not need a lot of supplies. The ideal growing area should have a temperature in the range of 65 °F to 70 °F and should not be hit by direct sunlight.

All you need is the following:

- White button mushroom spawn
- A box that is 14 inches by 16 inches and 6 inches deep
- A garbage bag
- Composted manure
- Newspaper
- Vermiculite

With the following steps, you will be able to see your white button mushrooms grow in no time:

1. Substrate preparation

- Line the box with the garbage bag. This makes the process less messy while still retaining moisture.
- Add a 50/50 mixture of composted manure and vermiculite to the box. The mix should be at most 3 inches deep.
- Wet the substrate with a little bit of water; it should only be damp.

2. Inoculation

- Inoculate the mixture using the white button mushrooms spawn. You only need about 50 grams of spawn per 11 pounds of substrate. Mix it into the first three inches of the substrate.
- Spray a bit of water into the newspaper and lay five layers on top of the spawn.
- Cover the box with a plastic bag, making sure to poke a few holes in it to help retain moisture.

3. Incubation

- It should take no more than three weeks for the mycelium to spread.
- Check at least once a day that the newspaper layers are moist enough. If not, spray a bit of water. Never pour water directly, as it might create wet areas that will stop the growth of the mycelium.

4. Fruiting

- To initiate the fruiting, add an additional mixture layer on top of your colonized mix of manure and vermiculite. Spray the new layer with water and cover everything with a plastic bag.
- Wait between three and five weeks for the pins to start forming. You will know the fruiting bodies are mature when the caps pop open.

5. Harvesting

- Harvest the white button mushrooms by twisting them out of the substrate.

And with that final step, we have reached the end of the 10 DIY projects, and the end of our book. It is now time for you to go and begin the wonderful journey of cultivating your own mushrooms.

CONCLUSION

The time has come for you to gather supplies, choose mushrooms, and get the equipment ready. You now hold the knowledge needed to begin cultivating mushrooms on your own. Gone are the days of shopping for mushrooms or foraging without properly knowing what to look for. Now, you can simply go outside or to your designated growing space and grab the mushrooms you want as soon as they are ready to be harvested.

Though putting theory into practice may seem slightly daunting, especially when your brain is filled with all of the information given to you in this book; once you get started you will find that the entire process is incredibly fun. You will learn much about yourself and nature, and even develop meaningful skills that can be carried over into other areas of your life. When growing your own mushrooms, you will find that it is not only about the end product, though mushrooms are a lovely reward, it is also about the process and the experiences you have. Growing mushrooms become much more than waiting for fruiting bodies to form. You develop a new outlook on fungi, their life cycles and their importance in nature. Knowing these things and seeing them in action is truly incredible; in the end, you reap the wonderful rewards of your hard work.

As we end this book you can now grow mushrooms for a number of reasons, including for culinary or medicinal purposes, because you are interested in growing a variety of mushrooms, or because you want easy access to more commonly used mushrooms like white buttons or shiitake. Or, perhaps you can embark on your mushroom cultivation journey because you like the look of mushrooms and are interested in their life cycle. Regardless of your motivation, you now have all the tools to create wonderful mushrooms. I wish you luck on your mushroom adventure and remember to have fun and find joy in every step along the way.

Made in the USA
Monee, IL
14 November 2023

45578238R00098